WHY I AM A MEMBER OF THE CHURCH OF CHRIST

LEROY BROWNLOW

THE BROWNLOW CORPORATION
FORT WORTH, TEXAS

To My Son
PAUL C. BROWNLOW

Fifty-Eighth Printing 2009
Copyright ©1945, Leroy Brownlow
Copyright renewed, 1973
The Brownlow Corporation
6309 Airport Freeway, Fort Worth, Texas 76117

ISBN 0-915720-71-X   Softcover
ISBN 0-915720-70-1   Hardcover

FOREWORD

BUT *sanctify in your hearts Christ as Lord: being ready always to give answer to every man that asketh you a reason concerning the hope that is in you, yet with meekness and fear."*—I Pet. 3:15.

The writer—believing this exhortation, and at the request of many in various localities who have heard him preach a series of sermons on this topic—presents to the public this volume of scriptural reasons for being a member of the church of Christ.

The most of the people are what they are religiously because of human rather than scriptural reasons. For instance: "It is a popular church"; "It is a friendly church"; "My mother was a member of that church"; "They got me when I was a baby by generation instead of regeneration"; "I married into this church"; "They have the finest building in town." Such reasons are worthless in the sight of God and are empty words to a people who wish to be guided by a "thus saith the Lord."

The author of this book was not reared in the church of Christ.

An effort has been made in this volume to set forth material that will be an asset to the children of God in preparing themselves to give answer to every man that asketh them a reason concerning the hope that is in them; material that may be used in home study to indoctrinate the children, for each generation must be indoctrinated; a book that may be circulated in the field of personal evangelism; a volume that will be helpful to those who make midweek talks; and a series of studies adapted to Bible class work.

A designated amount of material for each class period has not been prescribed, because different teachers cover

3

the same material at different paces. Being aware of this, the chapters have been broken into various sections and topics, making it easy for each class to cover the material at the speed it deems wise.

The writer does not claim originality in all the thoughts and arguments in this book. He has gleaned from many sources during his Christian life: college classes, lectures, sermons, debates, conversations, religious papers and many volumes of books. It is impossible for him to give honor to whom honor is due, but when direct quotations are used the author's name is given, together with the book or paper.

The church is "the pillar and ground of the truth" (I Tim. 3:15). The word of God is truth (Jno. 17:17). Thus, it is the responsibility of the church to teach and practice every truth in the word of God. That bases the teaching upon Biblical authority alone, rather than upon ecclesiastical authority as many religious bodies do. Hence, when we say the church of Christ teaches or practices a certain truth, it is understood that the church, by Biblical authority, is carrying out its divine mission as "the pillar and ground of the truth."

All Scripture quotations are from the American Standard Version, unless otherwise indicated.

The hope is now entertained that this volume of reasons for being a member of the church of Christ will be a source of light to those in darkness; a source of aid to those seeking Bible helps; and a source of glory to Him who will deal with all books according to their merits.

LEROY BROWNLOW

Fort Worth, Texas

4

CONTENTS

5

CONTENTS—Cont'd

REASON I

BECAUSE IT WAS FOUNDED BY THE SCRIPTURAL BUILDER—CHRIST

I. NO CHURCH CAN BE SCRIPTURAL UNLESS IT WAS FOUNDED BY THE SCRIPTURAL BUILDER

THE fact that a religious body exists is proof that it was founded by someone. There is in the world today a multiplicity of churches, different in origin, doctrine and practice; therefore, each was either scripturally or unscripturally founded by either the divine or a human builder. Hence, it is important to know whether the builder of a church was scriptural or unscriptural. If a church was founded by an unscriptural builder, that church must of necessity be unscriptural: the work of man and not of Christ.

II. CHRIST FOUNDED THE SCRIPTURAL CHURCH

1. *In proof of the above statement* we quote the words of Christ, in which he promised to build the church: "And upon this rock I will build my church" (Matt. 16:18). Therefore, it is certain that no church can be the scriptural church unless it was founded by Christ. If a church was founded by Henry VIII, John Calvin, John Wesley, Joseph Smith, Jr., or any other human being, that church is unquestionably human.

2. *Jesus, in keeping with his promise to build his church, gave Peter the authority to state the terms of admission into it:* "I will give unto thee the keys of the king-

dom of heaven: and whatsoever thou shalt bind on earth shall be bound in heaven; and whatsoever thou shalt loose on earth shall be loosed in heaven" (Matt. 16:19). No human being ever had scriptural authority to say this, because no human being ever had scriptural authority to originate a church. This could only be said authoritatively by Him who has all authority in heaven and on earth, the founder of the scriptural church.

III. THE CHURCH WAS NOT ESTABLISHED BY JOHN THE BAPTIST

1. Many religionists assume that the church was established by John the Baptist. *But the fact that it was established by Christ is irrefutable proof that it was not established by John the Baptist* or any other human being.

2. *John was dead at the time Jesus promised to build the church.* In Matt. 14:10 we read of the execution of John: "And he [Herod] sent and beheaded John in the prison." Bear in mind that John was dead as we turn two chapters and come to Christ's promise in Matt. 16:18: "I will build my church." "Will build" is future tense; John was dead and the establishment of the church was in the future. John the Baptist was a great man and did a scriptural work—viz.: he was the forerunner who went before the Lord to prepare the people to receive him (Isa. 40:3; Mal. 3:1; Lk. 1:17). John did this, but he did not establish the church of the Bible, or any other church known to man.

3. *It cannot be proved that Jesus, in promising to build his church, was only promising to build an adjunct to what John had established.* That argument will not stand, for the simple reason that Jesus promised to build

8

his church from the foundation: " . . . upon *this rock* I will build my church . . . "

4. *John the Baptist was never a member of the church,* or a citizen of the kingdom of heaven. Jesus said, "Verily, I say unto you, Among them that are born of women there hath not arisen a greater than John the Baptist: yet he that is but little in the kingdom of heaven is greater than he" (Matt. 11:11). How was it possible for John to be one of the greatest born of women, but for one of the least in the kingdom or church to be his superior? This example will clarify it: In grammar school there is no greater than Bill, but the least in high school is greater than he; this is true because Bill is not in high school. So John the Baptist was not in the church or kingdom of heaven.

IV. OTHER PLANTS WILL BE ROOTED UP

The church of Christ was founded by Christ and the gates of hades shall not prevail against it; but other plants will be rooted up. The warning is too plain and the penalty is too severe for me to be a member of some church not planted by the Father. Jesus, in speaking of the religions founded upon the tradition of the elders, said, "Every plant which my heavenly Father planted not, shall be rooted up" (Matt. 15:13). This was during the law of Moses. God had planted the Hebrew religion, and other plants were to be rooted up. If God would uproot other plants under that system of worship, will he not do the same under the Christian system? We must admit that the standard has not been lowered; therefore, the warning may be applied under the Christian dispensation to present conditions. May we heed the warning sounded by the Lord.

9

REASON II

BECAUSE IT WAS FOUNDED ON THE SCRIPTURAL FOUNDATION

I. THE IMPORTANCE OF A GOOD FOUNDATION

IT is a recognized fact that *no building or institution can be stronger than the foundation on which it rests.* The strength of either is directly dependent on the foundation. No house built out of proportion with the foundation can stand long. A church is no exception: Its stability and benefits depend upon its foundation.

2. *The scriptural church must have the scriptural foundation;* otherwise it would not be scriptural. Thus no man can consistently claim membership in the scriptural church unless he is a member of the church founded upon the scriptural foundation.

II. WHAT IS THE ROCK OR FOUNDATION

1. *To determine the identity of the rock* we must determine the confession to which it refers. Peter had just confessed Christ: "Thou art the Christ, the Son of the living God" (Matt. 16:16). Jesus immediately confessed Peter: "And I also say unto thee, that thou art Peter ... " Christ then promised to build his church upon this rock. The rock, therefore, must refer either to Christ's confession of Peter or Peter's confession of Christ. Many have been led to think that it has reference to Peter, since the word "Peter" means a rock or stone. But the original language will not permit this interpretation because two

different words are used: "Thou art Peter [*Petros*] and upon this rock [*petra*] I will build my church" Matt. 16:18). Thus Jesus did not promise to build his church upon Peter (*Petros*) but upon the rock (*petra*) instead: the grand and glorious fact that Christ is the Son of God. Hence, the Lord's church has not been founded upon the weakness of human flesh, but upon the divinity and sonship of Christ.

2. Other passages bear out this interpretation: (1) "For other foundation can no man lay than that which is laid, which is Jesus Christ" (I Cor. 3:11). (2) "Being built upon the foundation of the apostles and prophets, Christ Jesus himself being the chief corner stone" (Eph. 2:20). (3) "The stone which the builders rejected is become the head of the corner" (Psalms 118:22). Jesus applied this prophecy to himself (Matt. 21:42). Peter also applied it to Christ (Acts 4:11). This proof is overwhelming!

III. THIS FOUNDATION WILL STAND

1. *The sublime foundation that Christ is the Son of God has stood and will continue to stand.* The malicious and combined attacks of the opposition have not been able to weaken it. The infidels, atheists, modernists and skeptics have raved and ranted, but Christ remains the Son of the living God. This rock may truly be compared to an anvil that has worn out many hammers. This foundation stands as securely and firmly today as ever.

2. *We now notice a contradictory example*: Voltaire once boastfully declared that there would not be a copy of the Bible on earth in a hundred years. It has been more than a hundred years since his blasphemous prophecy was

11

given, and it is no closer to fulfillment now than it was then. The same press on which this infidel prophecy was issued is now being used by the Geneva Bible Society. What a prophecy!

3. *But what about the institutions founded upon men?* They are resting upon the sand; the foundations are weak and they will ultimately fall. Christ's church will come through triumphantly, for it is resting on a tried stone, a sure foundation.

REASON III

BECAUSE IT WAS FOUNDED AT THE SCRIPTURAL PLACE—JERUSALEM

I. A CHURCH NOT FOUNDED AT THE SCRIPTURAL PLACE IS NOT THE SCRIPTURAL CHURCH

A NOTHER reason for being a member of the church of Christ is that it was founded in Jerusalem, the scriptural place. If a person should be a member of some church first founded in London or New York, he could not claim membership in the church of Christ; for Christ's church did not have its origin in London or New York. Man just cannot be a member of the scriptural church unless he is a member of the church founded at the scriptural place.

II. SOME PASSAGES WHICH POINT TO ITS ESTABLISHMENT

1. *We shall first read Isaiah's prophecy*: "And it shall come to pass in the latter days, that the mountain of Jehovah's house shall be established on the top of the mountains, and shall be exalted above the hills; and all nations shall flow unto it. And many peoples shall go and say, Come ye, and let us go up to the mountain of Jehovah, to the house of the God of Jacob; and he will teach us his ways, and we will walk in his paths: for out of Zion shall go forth the law, and the word of Jehovah from Jerusalem" (Isa. 2:2,3). From this prophecy we learn, first, that Jehovah's house was to be established in Jerusalem. Second, Jehovah's house would be exalted and all nations would

13

flow into it. Third, the time of fulfillment would be in the latter days. We must now learn the meaning of Jehovah's house. Paul speaks of "the house of God, which is the church of the living God ... " (I Tim. 3:15). So Jehovah's house is the church, and from this passage we learn when and where it was to be established—viz.: in the latter days at Jerusalem.

2. *In Micah 4:1,2 we find the same prophecy almost verbatim.*

3. *Zechariah also prophesied that the Lord's house or church was to be founded in Jerusalem*: "Therefore thus saith Jehovah: I am returned to Jerusalem with mercies: my house shall be built in it, saith Jehovah of hosts, and a line shall be stretched forth over Jerusalem" (Zech. 1:16). So once again the Holy Spirit taught that the church was to have its origin in Jerusalem.

4. In giving the worldwide commission, *Jesus taught that Jerusalem was the starting place*: "Thus it is written that the Christ should suffer, and rise again from the dead the third day; and that repentance and remission of sins should be preached in his name unto all the nations, beginning from Jerusalem. Ye are witnesses of these things, and behold, I send forth the promise of my Father upon you: but tarry ye in the city, until ye be clothed with power from on high" (Lk. 24:46-49). We would note: (1) Christ had to suffer and rise from the dead before repentance and remission of sins should be preached in his name. (2) The proclamation of this message was to begin in Jerusalem. (3) They were to tarry in Jerusalem until they were endued with power from on high. Jesus had previously promised the apostles this power which they were to receive from on high. It is evident from John 14:26; 15:26,27; 16:7,8

that the Comforter, the Holy Spirit, would not come until Jesus went away, and that when the Holy Spirit should come he would do a number of things—viz.: teach the apostles all things, bring to their remembrance what Jesus had said and convict the world of sin. This is the power for which the apostles were commanded to tarry in Jerusalem.

III. THE FULFILLMENT OF THESE PASSAGES

1. *The Holy Spirit was not to come until Jesus had gone away* (Jno. 16:7). The apostles saw him ascend out of their sight (Acts 1:9).

2. *The apostles were commanded to tarry in Jerusalem* (Lk. 24:49). After the apostles watched the Lord's ascension they returned unto Jerusalem (Acts 1:12), the appointed place; there they tarried.

3. *The apostles were to be clothed with power from on high* (Luke 24:49). In Acts 2:1-4 we read of the fulfillment of this promise: "And when the day of Pentecost was now come, they were all together in one place. And suddenly there came from heaven a sound as of the rushing of a mighty wind, and it filled all the house where they were sitting. And there appeared unto them tongues parting asunder, like as of fire; and it sat upon each one of them. And they were all filled with the Holy Spirit, and began to speak with other tongues, as the Spirit gave them utterance." The Holy Spirit was to come and we see that he did come in Jerusalem on Pentecost.

4. *The word of the Lord was to go forth from Jerusalem in the latter days* (Isa. 2:2,3; Micah 4:1,2). We have the fulfillment of this prophecy in Acts 2:14-42, in which a stirring sermon was preached in Jerusalem. This occurred in the latter days; for Peter quoted Joel's prophecy (Joel

15

2:28-32) as proof of that which was to come to pass in the latter days. Hence, this was the right place and the right time.

5. *Repentance and remission of sins were to be preached in the Lord's name, beginning at Jerusalem* (Lk. 24:47). Peter proclaimed such a message, saying, "Repent ye, and be baptized every one of you in the name of Jesus Christ unto the remission of your sins . . . " (Acts 2:38).

6. *The Lord's house (the church) was to be established in Jerusalem in the last days* (Isa. 2:2,3; Mic. 4:1,2; Zech. 1:16). And that is when and where it was established. Those who heard the gospel on Pentecost in Jerusalem, who believed, repented and who were baptized were added to it: "They then that received his word were baptized: and there were added unto them in that day about three thousand souls" (Acts 2:41). In verse forty-seven of the chapter we read that the Lord added to the church. This occurred in the last days for Peter quoted Joel's prophecy in proof of a thing that was to occur in the last days (Acts 2:17-21). Beginning with this occasion in Acts 2 we find the church spoken of as a reality while prior to this it is spoken of as a future institution. So, according to prophecies and their fulfillment, the church of Christ had its origin in Jerusalem. This is the church of which I am a member.

IV. PLANTING THE SAME CHURCH IN ANY COMMUNITY AND AGE IS DEPENDENT UPON SOWING THE SAME SEED INSTEAD OF CHURCH SUCCESSION

1. *There is nothing to gain in church succession.* Even if a man could trace an institution, year by year, back to its establishment, he would have no assurance that it was

the identical institution that existed in the beginning. Over a period of years, a church could so apostatize that it could no longer be the true church. Paul said that an apostasy, or falling away, would come. Let us read a few passages, please: (1) "I know that after my departing grievous wolves shall enter in among you, not sparing the flock; and from among your own selves shall men arise, speaking perverse things, to draw away the disciples after them" (Acts 20:29,30). (2) "Now we beseech you, brethren, touching the coming of our Lord Jesus Christ, and our gathering together unto him; to the end that ye be not quickly shaken from your mind, nor yet be troubled, either by spirit, or by word, or by epistle as from us, as that the day of the Lord is just at hand; let no man beguile you in any wise: for it will not be, except the falling away come first, and the man of sin be revealed, the son of perdition, he that opposeth and exalteth himself against all that is called God or that is worshipped; so that he sitteth in the temple of God, setting himself forth as God" (II Thess. 2:1-4). (3) "But the Spirit saith expressly, that in latter times some shall fall away from the faith, giving heed to seducing spirits and doctrines of demons, through the hypocrisy of men that speak lies, branded in their own conscience as with a hot iron; forbidding to marry, and commanding to abstain from meats" (I Tim. 4:1-3). The above quotations make it clear that an apostate church would grow out of the true church; therefore, any church which can be traced back to Jerusalem and Pentecost might be an apostate church. Thus those who attempt to prove church succession—if they should succeed—might only prove themselves members of an apostate church.

17

2. *We had better be interested in seeing if we are sowing the same seed sown by the apostles.* We are told in the parable of the sower that the word of God is the seed of the kingdom (Lk. 8:11). If we sow the same seed the apostles sowed, the same church will spring forth: "For whatsoever a man soweth, that shall he also reap . . . " (Gal. 6:7). Every seed produces after its kind. Sow oats and you will reap oats; sow wheat and you may harvest wheat; plant cotton and it will produce cotton; sow the pure seed of the kingdom and the true church will result. When the seed of the kingdom was planted back in the first century it did not produce a crop of "tists," "dists" and "ites." Neither will the seed of the kingdom produce such crops today. Therefore we must admit that such crops exist today because some seeds other than the seed of the kingdom have been sown. The word of God, the seed of the kingdom, produces Christians only; all other crops have been produced by other seeds.

3. *We now illustrate:* If all the growing wheat throughout the world should be destroyed, wheat would not be destroyed as long as it exists in the seed. The seed may be planted and another crop which is in all respects identical with the original will spring forth. In like manner, permit me to suggest that if all growing congregations of the true church should be destroyed by apostasy or persecution and should become extinct for a thousand years, the church of the Lord would not be destroyed as long as the word of God, the seed of the kingdom lasts—and this seed will last forever, for Jesus said, "Heaven and earth shall pass away: but my words shall not pass away" (Mk. 13:31). By sowing this identical seed in any community we may plant a congregation of disciples, identical in every respect

18

with the original. The church of Christ had its origin in Jerusalem, but the same church can be founded in any city or community by preaching the same gospel. A few years after the Lord's church had its origin in Jerusalem, Paul went to Corinth and planted it there. He said, "I planted; Apollos watered; but God gave the increase" (I Cor. 3:6). The same institution that was planted in Corinth can be planted in any section of the earth at any time, provided man is careful to plant the same seed. This is where our chief interest should lie.

REASON IV

BECAUSE IT WAS FOUNDED AT THE SCRIPTURAL TIME—THE PENTECOST FOLLOWING THE RESURRECTION OF CHRIST

I. INTRODUCTION

THE time of the establishment of the church was briefly presented in showing where the church was established. This being true, I shall not lead you into a lengthy discussion, proving this institution was founded on Pentecost. The chart should suffice. The array of Scriptures on it undoubtedly proves that Pentecost was the time.

Any church not founded on Pentecost is not the true church. This is one of the tests by which to determine whether a church is the true church or a counterfeit church. In looking for the scriptural church, look for the marks: *built by Christ; built on Christ; in Jerusalem; on Pentecost.* Any church which does not bear these marks is not the church that Jesus promised to build. It may have many good people in it and may teach and do many excellent things, but it is not the church of the living God; it is a human church imposed on the credulity of man.

Isa.2:2-4 → Mic.4:1-2 → Dan.2:44 → Matt.3:1-2 → Mk.1:15 → Matt.6:9,10 → Matt.16:18 → Mt.9:1 → Matt.16:28 → Mk.10:19 → Mk.22nd →

Isa.2:2-4	Latter days in Jerusalem
Mic.4:1-2	Latter days in Jerusalem
Dan.2:44	In the days of those kings
Matt.3:1-2	Is at hand
Mk.1:15	Is at hand
Matt.6:9,10	Were to pray for its coming
Matt.16:18	Will build
Mt.9:1	Come in lifetime of some of the disciples
Matt.16:28	Disciples had not entered it
Mk.10:19	High unto you
Mk.22nd	Shall come

Pentecost

Acts 2:47 → Col.1:13,18 →

Added to it — Citizens of kingdom

1. Three thousand added that day (Acts 2:41).
2. Was in the last days (Acts 2:17-21).
3. Was at Jerusalem (Lk.24:46-49; Acts 1:12; 2:1-5).
4. Was in the days of those kings.
5. Was in the days of some of those disciples (Acts 1:15-2:9).
6. Power came (Acts 2:1-4).
7. The beginning was when the Holy Spirit came on the apostles (Acts 11:15). The Holy Spirit came on Pentecost.
8. The Scriptures point both forward to its coming and backward to its having come on Pentecost.

REASON V

BECAUSE CHRIST IS THE FOUNDER OF ONLY ONE CHURCH—HIS CHURCH

I. THE PROOF

HE who has all authority in heaven and on earth said, *"Upon this rock I will build my church . . ."* (Matt. 16:18). Jesus did not say that he would build a church, his churches or one of his churches. He said, "I will build my church." Let us spell it: C-H-U-R-C-H—that is how many Jesus promised to build. Everyone who knows anything at all about the English language as to whether nouns are singular or plural knows that the word "church" is singular and means one. It is hard for many good people, in view of present conditions, to be convinced of the oneness of the church; but, the multiplicity of churches about us has no power to alter the words of Christ. He declares: "My words shall not pass away" (Matt. 24:35).

2. *Paul teaches that there is one body*: "There is one body and one Spirit, even as also ye were called in one hope of your calling" (Eph. 4:4). "For even as we have many members in one body, and all the members have not the same office: so we, who are many, are one body in Christ, and severally members one of another" (Rom. 12:4,5). "But now they are many members, but one body" (I Cor. 12:20). Paul, as we see, has taught time after time the oneness of the body. Does the body mean the church? We shall see: "And he put all things in subjection under

his feet, and gave him to be head over all things to the church, which is his body'' (Eph. 1:22,23). In this passage Paul tells us that the church is the body. In Col. 1:18 he teaches that the body is the church. So the church is the body and the body is the church. There is only one body; therefore there is only one church. How perfectly this agrees with the promise: "I will build my church" (Matt. 16:18).

3. The oneness of the church is also seen in *the figure of a vineyard, with God the husbandman* (Jno. 15:1). We do not see the picture of many vineyards, being worked by the husbandman in such a way as to conflict with the welfare and growth of each. There are hundreds of religious vineyards in the world today, each claiming God as its husbandman. This is what we see when we lift up our eyes and look at the world, but this is not what we see when we look in the Bible. In it we see one vineyard and one husbandman.

4. This idea of the church is further portrayed in *the figure of the vine and branches*: Christ the true vine and each redeemed person a branch in the vine (Jno. 15:1-6). We do not see Christ as a plurality of vines with many branches in each vine, each vine and its branches growing in such a way as to conflict with the growth of others. No! This is not what we see at all. We see one great and beautiful vine, Christ, the Son of God, with every saved person a branch in him, saved by him and bearing fruit to his honor and glory. How contradictory is the picture of the world and the picture of the Bible!

Man in his desperate attempt to justify denominationalism has tried to tell us that the vine is the original and true church and the branches are the different denominations of the world. This is their number-one argument in behalf of denominationalism. A little thinking, however, will reveal that this cannot be true for several reasons: (1) Christ was speaking to his disciples instead of churches when he said, "I am the vine and ye are the branches" (Jno. 15:5). It is maltreatment of his word to apply a statement to churches when he applied it to men. (2) Christ said, "Abide in me," the true vine. If you are abiding in some branch, then you are guilty of error. Christ did not say, "Abide in some branch"; he said, "Abide in me." (3) He plainly states that a branch is a man: "If a man abide not in me he is cast forth as a branch." " . . . a man . . . is . . . a branch." English language could not make it plainer. (4) It cannot be true for it does an injury to the parable. It is preposterous and ridiculous to think that on the true vine grow a grape, a watermelon, cucumber, cantaloupe, pumpkin, squash, etc. Thinking persons could never accept a thing as sensible in the spiritual world when it is wholly and unreservedly nonsensical in the natural world; however there is no nonsense so nonsensical as the argument of a theologian who has no Scripture to prove his doctrine.

5. The unity of the church is also presented in *the figure of a house or family*: "the house of God, which is the church of the living God" (I Tim. 3:15). The house of God means the family of God. For instance, when we read of the jailer and his house being converted we know that it was the jailer and his family (Acts 16). Also, God's house is God's family; and God's family is God's church. We see in the Bible a vivid picture of a family with God as the Father, Christ the elder brother and all the saved as "children of God: and if children, then heirs; heirs of God, and

joint-heirs with Christ'' (Rom. 8:16,17). We do not see in the Bible a picture of several hundred different families, each more or less conflicting with all the others, each with a distinct government of its own, each wearing its own name, and each claiming the same Father and the same Elder Brother, with each child in every family claiming to be an heir. This would be bigamy. Men ought not by word or deed cast such a reflection upon God. The divine picture is one great united family with God as the Father and Christ as the Elder Brother, and all members working together for the good of the family.

6. This idea of oneness is again portrayed in *the figure of the one fold and one shepherd*: ''And they shall become one flock, one shepherd'' (Jno. 10:16). We must look in the world instead of the Bible to see many flocks, each claiming to have the same shepherd. God does not picture in his word hundreds of flocks, each with its peculiar kind of sheep, and each more or less at variance with all the others. God says: ''One flock, one shepherd.'' All the brains, all the wealth, and all the prestige of all the world cannot change his word. There are no more flocks than there are shepherds. It would be just as scriptural to ask a man which shepherd he is following as it would to ask him of which flock he is a member.

7. Consider another figure, please: this time, *the figure of the human body.* The church is presented in the figure of a human body with Christ as the head and all the redeemed as members of the body, working under the control and direction of the head (I Cor. 12:12-27; Col. 1:18). One body and one head. In the religious world we see hundreds of bodies, each claiming to have the one head, Christ. What a picture! What a beast! or shall we call it a beast?

25

It has no name for it was never heard of in the natural world. It has hundreds of bodies and each body fights all other bodies, and yet each body is guided and directed by the intelligence of one head. Do not get scared—you will never see that kind of a thing in the animal kingdom. But you can see hundreds of warring bodies in the religious world, each claiming to have Christ as its head. Surely, a man has eyes with which he cannot see and ears with which he cannot hear when he accepts this thing as reasonable in the religious world, knowing that it is unreasonable in the natural world.

8. The oneness and unity of God's people is further taught in *Christ's prayer unto the Father*. Let us study it for a moment: "Neither for these only do I pray, but for them also that believe on me through their word; that they may all be one; even as thou, Father, art in me, and I in thee, that they may also be in us: that the world may believe that thou didst send me" (Jno. 17:20,21). Jesus prayed that all who believe on him may be one. This prayer is a cutting rebuke to a plurality of churches. We know that Jesus did not pray for oneness and then turn around and establish many churches to create division. Such fickleness would be the blackest work of hypocrisy. Every time a man says that Jesus is the author of many churches, doctrines and divisions, he accuses the Lord of hypocrisy. It is equivalent to saying that Jesus was not sincere and honest when he went to the Father in prayer in the behalf of oneness. It is an accusation against the purity and integrity of our Redeemer. I cannot appreciate a man's casting that reflection upon my Saviour.

Many men have prayed for division. Oh, how many times we have seen preachers go down upon their knees in prayer and have heard them thank God that there are so many churches and doctrines in the world that each person may pick out the one of his choice. This is not the way Jesus prayed. Thus many have drifted far from the spirit of Christ.

II. A PLURALITY OF CHURCHES

Yes, the Bible speaks of "churches of Christ" (Rom. 16:16) and "the seven churches that are in Asia" (Rev. 1:4). The word *churches* is here used in a *congregational* sense. This usage is extant on every hand. We speak of the churches of Christ in the county, but they are all alike, having the same marks of identity. We speak of the seven or any number of churches in a certain territory just as the Holy Spirit spoke of "the seven churches that are in Asia."

This should be enough to convince the most incredulous that Christ is the founder of only one church. This being true, we have no choice in the matter and should be content to be members of Christ's church.

REASON VI

BECAUSE IT IS SCRIPTURAL IN NAME

I. IS THERE ANYTHING IN A NAME

THE idea that there is nothing in a name is a prevalent and popular doctrine, in keeping with neither Scripture nor reason.

1. There is so much in a name that *God named Adam and Eve.* He "called their name Adam, in the day when they were created" (Gen. 5:2). There is something in a name or God would not have named them.

2. If there is nothing in a name, explain why *God changed Abram's name to "Abraham" and Sarai's name to "Sarah"* (Gen. 17:5,15). There is so much in a name that God changed their names.

3. Again, there is so much importance attached to a name that *God changed Jacob's name to "Israel"* (Gen. 32:27,28). To say that there is nothing in a name is but to reflect upon the wisdom of God and accuse Him of doing foolish and useless acts.

4. *Paul condemned human and divisive names* by asking, "Is Christ divided? was Paul crucified for you? or were ye baptized into the name of Paul?" (I Cor. 1:13). Then why take Paul's name or some other man's name? Paul said, "I thank God that I baptized none of you, save Crispus and Gaius"—not that he underestimated the importance of baptism—but, "lest any man should say that ye were baptized into my name" (I Cor. 1:14,15). If

28

there is nothing in a name why did Paul condemn human names?

5. *A name is so meaningful* that men name their dogs "Fido" and "Satan"; their donkeys, "Rebel" and "Lucifer"; and their sons, "James" and "John." If there is nothing in a name, why not reverse the order and name the boys "Fido" and "Lucifer"?

6. If you still doubt that there is something in a name, *suppose you call a good American "Judas," "traitor" or "arsonist," or call a truthful man a "liar," or call a good citizen a "criminal,"* and it will not take you long to learn that, after all, there is something in a name.

II. WHAT THE CHURCH WAS CALLED

The church has no special name, but is spoken of in several significant appellations. It is called:

1. *"My church"* (Matt. 16:18). Jesus said that; therefore it is Christ's church.

2. *"The church"* (Acts 8:1). The word "church" comes from the Greek word "ekklesia," meaning a group of called-out people. The Lord has but one such group and it is called "the church."

3. *"Church of God"* (I Cor. 1:2). This shows ownership. For example, the house of Mr. Brown is the house belonging to Mr. Brown.

4. *"Churches of Christ"* (Rom. 16:16). The writer is speaking of the various local churches or congregations. This designates them as belonging to Christ.

5. *"The body of Christ"* (Eph. 4:12). The body which belongs to Christ.

6. *"The church of the living God"* (I Tim. 3:15). Indicates ownership.

29

7. *"Church of the firstborn"* (Heb. 12:23). The church of those who first received the gospel of Christ, firstborn, or first-fruits.

The members of the churches of Christ speak of the church in scriptural terms. What about other groups? You may see for yourself by looking over the doors of the meeting houses. You will see names not to be found in the Bible. It is strange that people who claim to be religious will wear some name or designation that is foreign to the Bible. Is this not a dishonor to God, Christ and the Bible?

III. WHAT THE MEMBERS WERE CALLED

We find that the members wore several distinctive and significant names, namely:

1. *"Disciples"* (Acts 20:7). This means learners or followers. It is a common noun and needs to be qualified to make known whom they are following. We read of the disciples of John (Matt. 9:14), disciples of the Pharisees (Mk. 2:18), and the disciples of Moses (Jno. 9:28), as well as the disciples of Christ.

2. *"Saints"* (I Cor. 1:2). Were called this because they were saved from past sins, were holy in life, and were sanctified or set apart by the gospel of Christ.

3. *"Beloved of God"* (Rom. 1:7). The dearly loved of God.

4. *"Brethren"* (I Cor. 15:6). Shows their relationship to each other. Men can be brethren in the flesh, in clubs, and in orders without being brethren in Christ; but they were brethren in Christ.

5. *"Sons of God"* (Rom. 8:14). They were called this in view of their relationship to God.

30

6. *"Children of God"* (I Jno. 3:1). Shows relationship to God.

7. *"Heirs of God"* (Rom. 8:17). This shows that they are to inherit from God.

8. *"Royal priesthood"* or "priests" (I Pet. 2:9). Each Christian is a priest in that he can "offer up spiritual sacrifices, acceptable to God through Jesus Christ," the High Priest (I Pet. 2:5; Heb. 8:1,2).

9. *"Christians"* (Acts 11:26). This is a proper noun and needs no qualifying words to make the distinction clear. The n me expresses the saved person's relationship to Christ.

(1) Some have tried to minimize the importance of this name, saying that it was used only in derision. But this name was given by divine authority. Isaiah prophesied: "And the nations [the Gentiles, K. J. V.] shall see thy righteousness, and all kings thy glory; and thou shalt be called by a new name, which the mouth of Jehovah shall name" (Isa. 62:2). They were not to be given this new name until after the Gentiles had been converted or had seen the righteousness of God. In Acts 10 we read of the conversion of the Gentiles: Cornelius and his household. In the next chapter (Acts 11:26) we read, "the disciples were ca ed Christians first in Antioch." This was a new name and it was given after the Gentiles had seen the righteousness of God. If this is not the new name that was to be given by Jehovah, then tell us what is, please.

(2) fter Paul had preached to King Agrippa the king exclaimed, "With but little persuasion thou wouldest fain make me a Christian" (Acts 26:28). This is what Paul tried to get every person to become and be. Reader, the Holy Spirit would not have you to be anything else!

31

(3) Peter says, "If a man suffer as a Christian, let him not be ashamed: but let him glorify God in this name" (I Pet. 4:16). We cannot glorify God in this name by wearing some other name. This is a positive command and those who disobey are guilty of sin.

(4) There are many other names under heaven and among men, but read Acts 4:12: "And in none other is there salvation; for neither is there any other name under heaven, that is given among men, wherein we must be saved." What an awful warning! Are you willing to heed it?

IV. HYPHENATED CHRISTIANS

I am sure that method and system should be used in the Lord's work, but I am not a Methodist; that we should have bishops (the Greek word being episcopos) to oversee the work in a congregation, but I am not an Episcopalian; that we should have elders (the Greek word being presbuteros) who are bishops to rule and oversee in the congregation, but I am not a Presbyterian; that each congregation is independent, but I am not a Congregationalist; that it takes immersion to constitute the act of baptism, but I am not a Baptist; that Christians should be holy but I am not a Holiness; that Christ will come again, but I am not an Adventist; that the church is universal or catholic, but I am not a Catholic. According to some good folk—since I believe in the above facts—I should call myself a *Methodist - Episcopalian - Presbyterian - Congregationalist - Baptist - Holiness - Catholic - Christian*. A monstrous hyphenation and a rather long name! It is unnecessary, too. We find in the Bible that the disciples were called Christians, but we never read of any person being called some hyphenated

Christian. Regardless of what names others wear, I prefer to stick to the Bible and be a Christian only.

V. TESTIMONY OF SPURGEON AND LUTHER

1. Listen to the language of *Charles Spurgeon,* the most recognized and talented Baptist preacher that ever lived: "I say of the Baptist name, let it perish, but let Christ's name last forever. I look forward with pleasure, to the day when there will not be a Baptist living. I hope they will soon be gone. I hope the Baptist name will soon perish; but let Christ's name endure forever."—*Spurgeon Memorial Library,* Vol. 1, p. 168.

2. Hear the words of *Martin Luther,* a man in whose name many people glory: "I pray you to leave my name alone, and call not yourselves Lutherans, but Christians. Who is Luther? My doctrine is not mine. I have not been crucified for anyone. St. Paul would not let any call themselves after Paul, nor of Peter, but of Christ. How then, does it befit me, a miserable bag of dust and ashes, to give my name to the children of God? Cease, my dear friends, to cling to these party names and distinctions: away with all; and let us call ourselves only Christians after him from whom our doctrine comes."—*The Life of Luther,* by Stork, p. 289.

Thus we see that in wearing human names, men displease not only God but the men they attempt to glorify.

VI. SYLLOGISMS

Perhaps it will be plainer if we shall put down some thoughts in the form of premises and then draw the conclusions:

1. *Syllogism one*:

(1) The Bible condemns human names (I Cor. 1:12, 13).

(2) The name "Lutheran" is a human name.

(3) Therefore, the name "Lutheran" is under condemnation.

2. *Syllogism two*:

(1) The Bible teaches that party names are carnal (I Cor. 3:3,4).

(2) The name "Methodist" is a party name.

(3) Therefore, the name "Methodist" is carnal.

3. *Syllogism three*:

(1) "Faith cometh by hearing, and hearing by the word of God" (Rom. 10:17).

(2) The name "Episcopal Church" is not in the word of God.

(3) Therefore, the name "Episcopal Church" is not of faith.

4. *Syllogism four*:

(1) Religious work is to be done in the name of the Lord (Col. 3:17).

(2) Presbyterians do religious work in the name of "Presbyterian."

(3) Therefore, the Presbyterians are guilty of error.

5. *Syllogism five*:

(1) Man is commanded to glorify God in the name "Christian" (I Pet. 4:16).

(2) Catholics are trying to glorify God in the name "Catholic."

(3) Therefore, Catholics are in disobedience to the command of God.

6. *Syllogism six:*

(1) There is salvation in no other name (Acts 4:12).

(2) The name "Baptist" is another name.

(3) Therefore, there is no salvation in the name "Baptist."

The names in the minor premises are used as examples. Many other names could have been used and the conclusions would have been the same. If the major and minor premises are true—and they are true—the conclusions are true. We plead with the good people of the world to repudiate all human, divisive and unscriptural names. The plea is meeting with success: thousands are giving up the unscriptural for the scriptural.

VII. TITLES

In the long ago the Jews corrupted their speech by using "half the speech of Ashdod" (Neh. 13:23,24). Figuratively speaking, we have much of the language of Ashdod in the world today. Many self-exalting titles are now being used in opposition to the teachings of the Bible.

1. *"Reverend."* The word *reverend* is found only one time in the English translation of the Bible; however, it is found many times in the original language. But it is not used as a title for man. For a person to apply this as a title to himself when the Holy Spirit never used the word in this manner is but to be guilty of perverting the Word. There is no mention in the Scriptures of "Reverend Paul," "Right Reverend James" and "The Right Reverend Peter." They looked upon themselves as weak creatures, needing the help of God, and refused "to glory, save in the cross of our Lord Jesus Christ" (Gal. 6:14). Some preachers speak of Paul as plain Paul, James as just plain James,

John as just plain John and Jesus as just Jesus, but speak of themselves and other preachers as "Reverend So-and-So." This would be comical, if it were not so tragic. Even Jesus, while living in the flesh on the earth, refused the title of "Good" (Matt. 19:16,17). Paul began some of his letters in these words: "Paul, a servant of Jesus Christ." Paul described himself simply as "a servant" or "a bond-servant." But many uninspired preachers of today affix the most sacred and highest terms possible to their names. What a contrast! The desire for high-sounding titles grows out of the desire to be exalted. We are reminded of the pertinent words of Jesus: "Whosoever would become great among you shall be your minister: and whosoever would be first among you shall be your servant." (Matt. 20:26,27).

2. *"Pastor."* The minister or evangelist of the church is not a pastor unless he has been appointed to "the office of a bishop," overseer or elder. The New Testament provides for a plurality of bishops, overseers, elders or pastors in each congregation (Acts 14:23). They are to exercise a pastor's or shepherd's watchfulness in protecting the flock. These words are not titles, but are nouns like "rancher," "teacher," "farmer" and "carpenter."

3. *"Father."* This word is often used as a religious title in direct opposition to the teaching of Christ: "And call no man your father on the earth: for one is your Father, even he who is in heaven" (Matt. 23:9). This is speaking of a religious usage rather than a physical relationship, because the Holy Spirit often uses the word "father" in speaking of one's parents. Is it not strange that millions will use a title that is positively forbidden by Christ?

The church of Christ is scriptural in name and language. No man can deny it. It is the belief and practice of the church of Christ to call "Bible things by Bible names." Paul exhorted Timothy to do this, saying, "Hold the pattern of sound words" (II Tim. 1:13). We should avoid the popular tendency to bestow flattering titles, but should rather follow this advice: "Let me not, I pray you, respect any man's person; neither will I give flattering titles unto any man. For I know not to give flattering titles" (Job 32:21, 22).

REASON VII
BECAUSE IT IS SCRIPTURAL IN ORGANIZATION

I. ECCLESIASTICISMS

THE denominations are ruled by their ecclesiastical forms of government. They have ignored the head of the church and have assumed the right of self-government. They confess with the mouth that Christ has "all authority," but the heart is far from it and is set on a democratic form of government. Therefore, we hear much of "synods," "presbyteries," "councils," "general assemblies" and "conferences." In these delegations men legislate rules and laws to govern the various ecclesiasticisms.

2. *Of course this power to legislate was never given to any group of uninspired men.* No group of men has authority from the Bible to decide how many times a year the Lord's supper is to be taken, to change the act of baptism, to set aside baptism as a condition of salvation, or to make any other changes in the divine order. Any man who has assumed the authority to change the government of the church or the laws given by the apostles has rebelled against Christ, the head and supreme authority. Christ's will is law and rebellion against it is treason.

3. *A rejection of the supreme authority of Christ is the outgrowth of modifications.* One alteration led to others, and finally human heads over religious groups evolved. A change in organization leads to a change in laws; this change in laws dethrones Christ as King and inaugurates a human authority to reign and rule.

38

II. A MONARCHY

1. *Christ's church is a monarchy.* He is the supreme head. "And he is the head of the body, the church; who is the beginning, the firstborn from the dead; that in all things he might have the preeminence" (Col. 1:18). Listen to Paul again: "And he put all things in subjection under his feet, and gave him to be head over all things to the church, which is his body, the fulness of him that filleth all in all" (Eph. 1:22,23). At the transfiguration God said, "This is my beloved Son, in whom I am well pleased; hear ye him" (Matt. 17:5). Shortly before Christ ascended to the right hand of God, he said, "All authority hath been given unto me in heaven and on earth" (Matt. 28:18). Christ has all authority; therefore man has none. Christ will not abolish "all rule and all authority and power" until the end comes (I Cor. 15:24).

2. *Jesus promised to send the apostles the Holy Spirit,* who was to teach them all things, and bring all things to their remembrance, whatsoever he had said to them (Jno. 14:26). The Holy Spirit was to testify of Christ and the apostles were to bear witness (Jno. 15:26,27). The teaching and testimony of the apostles would be sanctioned in heaven, for "whatsoever thou shalt bind on earth shall be bound in heaven; and whatsoever thou shalt loose on earth shall be loosed in heaven" (Matt. 16:19). Christ never delegated this authority to any others than the apostles. For men this side of the apostles in their conventions, councils, and synods to assume such authority is but an insult to the King on his throne.

III. THE AUTONOMY OF THE CHURCH

1. In speaking of the autonomy of the church *we mean the autonomy of the local church or congregation.* Auton-

omy is defined as "right of self-government; a self-governing state; an independent body." In the first century each congregation was such. Each was independent of every other congregation. There was no tyranny of one church over another. The church in Rome or Jerusalem had no authority over the churches in other communities. Men outside the congregation had no right to exercise authority and power within the congregation. The elders and deacons in one congregation had no authority to exercise despotic rule or any other kind of rule over the elders and deacons in another congregation. Each church was free and independent, under the teaching of Christ and the apostles, to govern itself, carry on its own work, and manage its own affairs. There was no system of church government larger or smaller than the congregation. All congregations had the same head, foundation, and mission; preached the same gospel; constituted the one body. But each was independent to direct its own work!

2. *"The wisdom of God is seen in such an arrangement for his churches.* If one became corrupted in doctrine or affected by evil practices, other churches would not be so affected. If dissension arose in one, it would not spread to the others; if one perished, the others would not be dragged down. If a window is made of one large pane, a break injures the entire pane; but if it be made of several panes, it is not so bad to break one. The independence of the churches is a protection for each one."—H. Leo Boles, *Gospel Advocate,* Feb. 15, 1940.

3. *This simple organization, however, failed to satisfy many.* Hence, they made changes whereby their unchristian aspirations for ecclesiastical lordship could be realized.

History records the first great departure from the truth in the system of church government.

IV. ELDERS

1. *The Holy Spirit has taught that elders, bishops, overseers or pastors be ordained in every church* (Titus 1:5). In Acts 20:17 we read that Paul "called to him the elders of the church." In speaking to this group Paul declared that they were bishops (American Standard Version) or overseers (King James Version, Acts 20:28). Men who did this work are also spoken of as pastors (Eph. 4:11). So in each church there is to be a plurality of elders or bishops—not a plurality of churches to one bishop. In ecclesiasticisms men have completely reversed this divine arrangement and have many churches to one bishop.

2. *It is the duty of bishops to* (1) "take heed unto" (a) themselves and (b) "all the flock"; (2) "feed the church of the Lord" (Acts 20:28); (3) "help the weak" (Acts 20:35); "exhort in the sound doctrine" and (5) "convict the gainsayers" (Titus 1:9); (6) "admonish the disorderly," (7) "encourage the fainthearted," (8) "be longsuffering toward all" (I Thess. 5:14); (10) exercise "the oversight, not of constraint, but willingly, according to the will of God; nor yet for filthy lucre, but of a ready mind, neither as lording it over the charge alloted to" them, but (11) make themselves "as ensamples to the flock" (I Pet. 5:2,3); (12) visit the sick (Jas. 5:14); (13) "watch in behalf" of the souls of the members (Heb. 13:17). The above-stated duties have been imposed upon them by the Lord. When this work is not performed, the congregaton suffers. There is not the least intimation in all the Bible that the elders have divine authority to nullify or modify

41

the law of Christ. They have only the authority to enforce Christ's law, and not to make laws to govern their charges. Blessed is the congregation which has elders who perform the aforesaid duties.

3. *The qualifications of a bishop are as follows:* (1) "The bishop therefore must be without reproach," (2) "the husband of one wife," (3) "temperate," (4) "sober-minded," (5) "orderly," (6) "given to hospitality," (7) "apt to teach"; (8) "no brawler," (9) "no striker"; (10) "but gentle" (11) "not contentious," (12) "no lover of money" (13) "one that ruleth well his own house, having his children in subjection with all gravity; (but if a man knoweth not how to rule his own house, how shall he take care of the church of God?)" (14) "not a novice, lest being puffed up he fall into the condemnation of the devil"; (15) "moreover he must have good testimony from them that are without" (I Tim. 3:2-7); (16) "having children that believe"; (17) "not self-willed," (18) "not soon angry," (19) "a lover of good," (20) "just," (21) "holy," (22) "self-controlled"; (23) "holding to the faithful word which is according to the teaching" (Titus 1:6-9). Too frequently the work of a bishop is given to men who have not the qualifications, and who assume this responsibility with little realization of their duties.

4. *The congregation is commanded* (1) "to know them that labor among you, and are over you in the Lord, and admonish you"; (2) "and to esteem them exceeding highly in love for their work's sake" (I Thess. 5:12, 13); (3) "let the elders that rule well be counted worthy of double honor, especially those who labor in the word and in teaching" (I Tim. 5:17); (4) "obey them that have the rule over you," (5) "and submit to them" (Heb. 13:17);

(6) "against an elder receive not an accusation, except at the mouth of two or three witnesses" (I Tim. 5:19). It is just as essential that the congregation measure up to its duties toward the elders as it is for the elders to perform their duties toward the congregation.

V. DEACONS

1. *The duties of deacons* are not as clear-cut as the duties of the elders, but they were undoubtedly that of helpers and servants. In Acts 6:1-6 we read of seven men in the church at Jerusalem appointed to "serve tables." This group is not identified in the Bible as deacons, but from the original language we learn that they did the work of deacons or servants, the word "deacons" meaning servants. Thus the elders are the rulers or overseers and the deacons are servants. It has been said that the work of elders was spiritual and the work of deacons was physical, but their works cannot be limited to these spheres. We cannot say that the elders as rulers in the congregation should have nothing to do with finances, for we read in Acts 11:29, 30 of a contribution being sent to the elders in Jerusalem by the hand of Barnabas and Saul. Neither can we say that the deacons' work is limited to physical matters, for we find that Stephen and Philip, two of the seven selected at Jerusalem, later preached the gospel with much force and persuasion.

2. *Those who are selected to do this work must have the following qualifications:* (1) "men of good report," (2) "full of the Spirit" (3) "and of wisdom" (Acts 6:3); (4) "must be grave"; (5) "not double-tongued," (6) "not given to much wine," (7) "not greedy of filthy lucre"; (8) "holding the mystery of the faith in a pure con-

science''; (9) "first be proved''; (10) "be blameless'';
(11) "even so must their wives be grave, not slanderers, so-
ber, faithful in all things'' (King James Version); (12)
"husbands of one wife,'' (13) "ruling their children and
their own houses well'' (I Tim. 3:8-12).

Church organization is simple, but the divine plan has
been greatly abused. Every attempt to improve this
plan has resulted in apostasy and ecclesiasticism.

REASON VIII

BECAUSE IT HAS THE BIBLE AS ITS ONLY CREED, CONFESSION OF FAITH OR CHURCH MANUAL

I. REASONS FOR THIS CONVICTION

I COULD never become a participant in some religious system which has a human creed. This is my conviction for several reasons, namely:

1. *In the time of the apostles and for the first three centuries the Bible was the only creed.* Why not use the same creed today? I do not care to have a church manual similar to the one that existed in the first century. I want to have the same one. For this to be possible, I must have the Bible only.

2. *The Bible completely furnishes us unto every good work*: We know "that his divine power hath granted unto us all things that pertain to life and godliness, through the knowledge of him that called us by his own glory and virtue" (II Pet. 1:3); that "Every scripture inspired of God is also profitable for teaching, for reproof, for correction, for instruction which is in righteousness; that the man of God may be complete, furnished completely unto every good work" (II Tim. 3:16,17). The Holy Spirit says that the Scriptures have been given to furnish us unto doctrine, reproof, correction, instruction in righteousness, and unto every good work. Now, are not human creeds written to furnish man unto doctrine, reproof, correction, instruction in righteousness, and unto every good work? Yes. Then

why pledge allegiance to a human creed which has been given for the same purpose God gave the Bible? The Bible is safe, but are human creeds? Even their adherents admit that they are fallible. Why be an adherent to something that is of human origin and is fallible when you can be a follower of that which is of divine origin and is infallible? Even if the church leaders should write a creed which is not an addition to or a subtraction from the Bible, it would be exactly like the Bible. Why have two that are exactly alike? There would be no purpose in it.

3. *The following can be said of the Bible only:* "This old Book contains the mind of God, the state of man, the way of salvation, the doom of sinners and the happiness of believers. Its histories are true, its doctrines are holy, its precepts are binding, and its decisions are immutable. Read it to be wise, believe it to be safe, and practice it to be holy. It contains light to direct you, food to support you, and comfort to cheer you. It is the traveler's map, the pilgrim's staff, the sailor's compass, the soldier's sword, and the Christian's charter. Here paradise is restored, heaven is opened and the gates of hell are disclosed. Christ is its subject, our good its design, and the glory of God its end. It should fill the memory, rule the heart, and guide the feet. Read it slowly, frequently, prayerfully. It is a mine of wealth, a paradise of glory and a river of pleasure. It is given you in life, will be open at the judgment and will be remembered forever. It involves the highest responsibility, rewards the greatest labor and condemns all who trifle with its holy contents."—Anon. No man-made creed can make this claim. How unnecessary such creeds are!

4. *Human creeds are revised every few years because of their imperfection.* No disciple of a human creed knows

what his doctrine will be ten years hence. A church which had been teaching for years that children were born totally depraved changed its creed three or four years ago and began to teach that children are not born vile, vicious, corrupted and evil. The members who had supported the creed were called upon to have a rightabout-face. This is just one example. Creeds are constantly being changed and revised. This alone places upon them the stigma of weakness and imperfection.

While human creeds become obsolete and are discarded for new ones, the Bible continues to live and function. It lives because it needs no changing. The gospel of Christ is perfect and is spoken of as "the perfect law of liberty" (Jas. 1:25). It is perfect, and a curse of damnation rests upon any person or group of persons who would pervert it by adding to it or taking from it (Gal. 1:6-9; Rev. 22:18, 19). God's word is perfect and he has never permitted man to tamper with it. Even back in the time of Moses the Lord said, "Ye shall not add unto the word which I command you, neither shall ye diminish from it" (Deut. 4:2).

5. *Human creeds cannot be defended.* The following is a quotation from the works of Benjamin Franklin:

"First, any creed containing more than the Bible is objectionable, because it does contain more than the Bible.

"Second, any creed containing less than the Bible is objectionable, because it does contain less than the Bible.

"Third, any creed differing from the Bible is objectionable, because it does differ from the Bible.

"Fourth, any creed precisely like the Bible is useless, because we have the Bible.

"This covers the whole ground. There can be no other thought of. A creed must contain more than the Bible, less than the Bible, differ from it, or be precisely like it. No man defends his creed on the ground that it contains more than the Bible, less than the Bible, that it is different from the Bible, or precisely like it. If a creed be not defended on some of these grounds, on what ground can it be defended? Certainly on no ground conceivable to mortal man.''

6. *Those who have pledged allegiance to humanly written creeds are unable to defend the Bible.* Their position nullifies every word they say in the behalf of the completeness and perfection of the word of God. They are failing to show their faith by their works (Jas. 2:18). In fact, by their works they are showing their lack of faith in it. If a man will not take the Bible and it alone as his only creed, he cannot successfully defend it against the infidel. It is utterly impossible for a preacher to defend the teaching of the Bible when his own teaching is regulated by some book other than the Bible. This inconsistency is proof of his lack of confidence in it and appreciation of it. The infidel would say, ''Preacher, explain to us why you have some creed other than the Bible, if the Bible be true. If it is true, as you contend—given unto doctrine, reproof, correction, instruction in righteousness, and unto every good work—justify your human creed.'' You can picture the creed-bound preacher's confusion and embarrassment.

Over a hundred years ago, Robert Dale Owen of Scotland, the Goliath of infidelity, came to America. He did as the Goliath of the Philistines in the long ago; he defied the people of God; he begged the followers of Christ to send forth a man to engage him in polemic combat as to the truth of the Bible. The denominational, creed-bound preachers trembled at the sound of his challenge. Why?

They knew their position was hopelessly defenseless! They knew Owen would ask them to justify creeds other than the Bible; explain why they wore names not mentioned in the Bible; and make plain why they were members of churches foreign to the Bible. They trembled! But a David arose to accept the challenge. He was a Christian only, just a member of Christ's church and it alone, and had no creed but the Bible. The battle for truth was fought in Cincinnati, beginning April 13, 1829, and lasted for eight days. Mr. Owen, the Goliath of infidelity, was unable to use his favorite weapon: the inconsistency of those professing to believe the Bible and being at variance with it. His challenger was a member of no denomination, wore no human name and had no human creed. The infidel went down. It was a great victory for the Bible and Christian people were jubilant. This defender of the faith was Alexander Campbell. Many preachers could have done the same thing, if it had not been for their defenseless positions. Men cannot defend the Bible when they have pledged their support to the creeds written by uninspired men.

7. *Human creeds are divisive.* They keep religious people divided into parties and sects. Each creed serves as a wall to include and enclose its own adherents and to exclude all others. These walls must tumble and fall before unity can become a reality. All of them must go—one denomination cannot expect all other denominations to cast aside their human creeds to pledge support to another human creed. If they are going to follow a human creed, they will just keep the one they have. When human creeds are abolished, denominational barriers will begin to weaken and a divided people will be on the road to unity.

II. SYLLOGISMS

There is no doubt that division is sinful. Listen to the Holy Spirit's message: "Now I beseech you, brethren, through the name of our Lord Jesus Christ, that ye all speak the same thing and that there be no divisions among you; but that ye be perfected together in the same mind and in the same judgment" (I Cor. 1:10). Division is sinful, a violation of a positive command. Human creeds contribute to this sinful state; therefore, human creeds are sinful and those who support them share in the guilt of sin.

Perhaps it will be plainer if we set forth some premises and then draw the conclusions.

1. *Syllogism one:*
(1) Division is sinful (I Cor. 1:10; 3:3).
(2) Human creeds are divisive (openly admitted).
(3) Therefore, human creeds are sinful.

2. *Syllogism two:*
(1) It is sinful to walk by different rules (Phil. 3:16).
(2) Human creeds are different rules (admitted by all).
(3) Therefore, it is sinful to walk by human creeds.

3. *Syllogism three:*
(1) Division promotes infidelity (Jno. 17:20,21).
(2) Human creeds promote division (admitted by all).
(3) Therefore, human creeds promote infidelity.

The only way these conclusions can be disproved is to disprove either the major or minor premise. If the premises are true, the conclusions are unquestionable. They are true—thus the conclusions are certain.

REASON IX

BECAUSE IT BELIEVES ALL THE BIBLE TO BE THE INSPIRED WORD OF GOD

I. THE VIEWS OF A CROSS SECTION OF MINISTERS

IN a sermon on "Modern Attitudes Toward the Bible," by L. R. Wilson, (*Firm Foundation*, April 28, 1942) we have the following: "Only last year Dr. Clarence Edward McCartney, in a sermon on the 'The Glorious Gospel,' in a periodical called 'Preaching Today,' quoted statistics (from Betts, in a publication by the Abington Press, under the caption of "Beliefs of 700 Ministers") which showed the following results: Thirteen per cent rejected the doctrine of the Trinity; forty eight per cent rejected the Bible account of creation; thirty three per cent no longer believe there is a devil; thirty eight per cent do not believe in a revelation from God; forty three per cent reject the plenary inspiration of the Scriptures; thirty eight per cent do not believe the Old Testament prophets were able to predict future events; fifty five per cent do not believe the Bible is wholly free from myths and legends; nineteen per cent reject the account of the incarnation; nineteen per cent do not believe that Jesus is equal with God; twenty four per cent reject the atonement of Christ; twelve per cent reject the resurrection of Christ; thirty four per cent no longer believe in the future punishment of the wicked; thirty three per cent do not believe in the resurrection of the body; twenty seven per cent do not believe that Jesus will come again to judge the quick and the dead; thirty three per cent reject the fall of man as related in the book of Genesis; fifty one per cent regard baptism and the Lord's supper as non-essential; thirty nine per cent think that good, well-meaning persons should be received into the church regardless of their belief about salvation."

2. *It is amazing that so many do not believe the Bible to be the inspired and authoritative word of God;* hence, do not believe what God says on many subjects. The atheist is far more consistent than the modernist: The atheist does not believe any of the Bible while the modernist believes just what pleases him.

II. REASONS FOR BELIEVING THE BIBLE

Consider a few of the many reasons for believing the Bible:

1. *If the Bible is not true, then there is no acceptable and trustworthy history.* No other history has such characteristics of genuineness and reliability. The Bible bears every mark of authenticity. In speaking of Christ it was said, ". . . . that which we have heard, that which we have seen with our eyes that which we beheld, and our hands handled..." (I Jno. 1:1). The evidence is not hearsay—they had seen, heard, and touched Christ—and is acceptable from the viewpoint of knowledge. The fact that they had heard, seen and touched Christ is too much to be rejected on the assumption that they may have had poor vision, hearing or sense of touch. Their testimony is also acceptable from the standpoint of honesty and veracity. It is ridiculous to either accuse them of perjury or question their sincerity. It brought them no physical and temporal gain to give this testimony. It meant the giving up

of friends, home and an easy life; it meant persecution and death. It is absurd to say that men would die for something they knew to be a lie. No historian ever gave stronger proof of sincerity than they. If the Bible is not true, then there is no history that merits our acceptance.

> Whence but from heaven could men, unskilled in arts,
> In several ages born, in several parts,
> Weave such agreeing truths; or how or why
> Should all conspire to cheat us with a lie?
> Unmasked their pains, ungrateful their advice,
> Starvation their gains, and martyrdom their price.

2. The Bible, a book of books, sixty-six in number but one in harmony and thought, written by about forty different writers during intervals of about sixteen centuries, *could not have been written accidentally.* These men lived in different periods of history, followed different occupations, and labored under different customs, governments and geographical locations. They lived in different times and in different sections and wrote independently of each other. Hence, it is impossible for them to have conspired to write a pious fraud. But when their works were put together, we had one great volume of harmony and continuity of thought from the beginning to the end. This could not have accidentally occurred! It must have been superhuman and divine in its plan and the work of a Higher Power. We might as well argue that hundreds of workers and builders worked each after his own plan; and that without harmonious design or prearrangement, all their materials and efforts constructed the Empire State Building, as that the Bible is the work of chance.

3. *The fact that these men with a cross section of occupations, accomplishments and abilities have written a sublime and harmonious volume is unequivocal proof that*

53

these *"men spake from God, being moved by the Holy Spirit"* (II Pet. 1:21). For instance, Moses was educated in the wisdom of the Egyptians and was a shepherd and a leader; Joshua, a soldier and a spy; Ezra, a famous scribe and a pious priest; Nehemiah, cupbearer to the king; David, shepherd, musician, war hero and king; Solomon, the wisest man on earth and a powerful king; Isaiah, a prophet; Ezekiel, a Jewish exile; Daniel, a statesman; Amos, a shepherd and a peasant; Matthew, a tax collector; Peter and John, fishermen, "unlearned and ignorant men"; Luke, a physician; and Paul, a tentmaker and a scholar brought up at the feet of Gamaliel. Uninspired men who varied so widely in occupations and abilities could not have written a book that "is the hive of all sweetness, the armory of all well-tempered weapons, the tower containing the crown jewels of the universe, the lamp that kindles all other lights, the home of all majesties and splendors, the steppingstone on which heaven stoops to kiss the earth with its glories," a volume often questioned but never refuted. This could not be the work of chance! It must be the work of God!

4. *If the Bible is not true, error is worth more to the world than truth.* If it is not true, it is false—yet, it has done more to elevate man and bless the world than all the combined utterances of atheists, skeptics, agnostics, deists, higher critics and unitarians. The Bible has always been the axe that has cleared the pathway for the advancement of civilization. It has always been the purifying influence in human nature. The most sympathetic, virtuous and brotherly persons have embraced it as the truth. Hence,

if the Bible is not true, then the world is better off with a lie than with the truth.

5. *If the Bible is not true, "nature works in vain."* "Amongst earth's inhabitants there is one class of beings for whose creation and comfort all others do exist. Man is the name of that class of beings . . . If he be lost—for ever lost, all is lost. Crops of vegetables annually spring out of the earth, and return to it again. Races of animals feed upon them, and die. They, like their food, but enrich the earth. Day and night succeed each other. Years revolve. The earth turns upon its axis, wheels around its orbit, feeds and buries all its tenantry. Man himself and his food alike perish for ever.

"Now what is gained by the whole operation? If man lives not again—if the Bible be not true, nature labors in vain: and if there be a Creator, he works without a plan, and toils for no purpose . . . If, then, the Bible be not true—if the history it gives of man, his creation, his fall, his recovery, be not true—in one word, if the gospel be a lie and the Bible false, no living man can give one good reason for the existence of our planet."—*Christian Baptism*, Campbell. If the Bible is not true, man lives for no purpose, nature is a monstrous miscarriage, and the plan of the universe is a colossal failure.

6. An outstanding characteristic of the Bible, not found in other books, is that *it is authoritative in expression.* "Thus saith the Lord" is found nearly two thousand times. It claims to be from the Lord. It never uses means to prove statements. The statements are based upon the complete authority of God, its author. While human writers are doubtful and uncertain, the Bible is definite

and sure. It even speaks of the future as positively as if it were the past. This distinguishes it from human works.

7. The Bible is different from human books in that *it is not biased.* Man who is pictured on the highest plane is also described as the doer of the blackest sins. For an example: It is said that David was a man after God's own heart, but he is also described as an adulterer and murderer. Men are prone to give a one-sided biography. If he is a friend, they minimize his sins and magnify his virtues. If he be an enemy, they magnify his short comings and minimize his excellencies. But a distinctive characteristic of the Bible is that it "is no respector of persons." It speaks the whole truth concerning every man. How different from the works of men!

8. The Bible must be the work of God because of *the fulfillment of its prophecies.* We could use many prophecies relative to many subjects as an example, but we shall notice some concerning the Christ.

(1) It was prophesied that Christ would be born of a virgin (Isa. 7:13,14). It was fulfilled (Lk. 1:26-35).

(2) It was prophesied that Christ would be born in Bethlehem (Mic. 5:2). It came to pass (Matt. 2:1-11).

(3) It was predicted that a forerunner would prepare the way for the Lord (Isa. 40:3; Mal. 3:1,2). It was fulfilled as predicted (Jno. 1:22, 23; Mk. 1:1-7).

(4) We also have the prophecy that Jesus would ride into Jerusalem "upon an ass, and upon a colt the foal of an ass" (Zech. 9:9,10). It was fulfilled (Matt. 21:1-9).

(5) It was predicted that our Saviour would be betrayed by a familiar friend (Psa. 41:9). It is now history (Mk. 14:43-49).

(6) It was prophesied that the price of betrayal would be thirty pieces of silver and that the betrayer would return the sum (Zech. 11:12,13). We have a record of its fulfillment (Matt. 27:3-10).

(7) It was foretold that He would be scourged and mocked (Isa. 50:6). It is now history (Jno. 19:1; Mk. 14:65; Matt. 27:27-31).

(8) Isaiah prophesied that Jesus would suffer in silence as a lamb (Isa. 53:4-7). The prophecy stands fulfilled (Mk. 15:2-5).

(9) In Psa. 22:18 we have, "They part my garments among them, and upon my vesture do they cast lots." This came to pass (Jno.19:23,24).

Many other fulfilled Messianic prophecies could be given, but this should suffice. However, perhaps we should notice another prophecy of which we are witnesses to its fulfillment. Paul prophesied that some would depart from the faith and establish a system of religion in which men would be forbidden to marry and commanded to abstain from meats (I Tim. 4:1-3). The Roman Catholic Church has fulfilled this prophecy. They forbid certain ones to marry and command their members to abstain from meats on certain days and seasons. How did Paul know that this would come to pass? The only explanation is that he was guided by the Holy Spirit. There is no other way to explain the fulfillment of all the foretold events.

9. The divine inspiration of the Bible is fully proved by *its statements concerning the rotundity of the earth.* It was in 1543 that the Copernican theory that the earth is round and rotates upon its axis was advanced. But hundreds of years before man ever dreamed of such, God said,

"He stretcheth out the north over empty space, and hangeth the earth upon nothing" (Job. 26:7). No scientist ever gave a better description of the earth than this. Isaiah said, "It is he that sitteth upon the circle of the earth" (Isa. 40:22). No human being at this time would have spoken of the "circle of the earth," for man thought it was flat. Jesus, in speaking of his second coming, says that he will come in the day and in the night (Lk. 17:31, 34). For years this was a difficult passage. Men wondered how that Jesus could come both in the day and in the night. The enemies of the Bible claimed that it was a contradiction. But the passage is now easy since man has learned that it is day on one part of the earth while it is night on the other. Therefore, whenever Jesus comes, he will come in the day and in the night. This truth was put in the Bible hundreds of years before man ever dreamed of such. How are we going to account for it? There is but one answer: the writer was guided by a Higher Power.

10. *Josephus confirms the truths of the Bible concerning Christ:* "Now there was about this time Jesus, a wise man, if it be lawful to call him a man; for he was a doer of wonderful works, a teacher of such men as receive the truth with pleasure. He drew over to him both many of the Jews and many of the Gentiles. He was (the) Christ. And when Pilate, at the suggestion of the principal men amongst us, had condemned him to the cross, those that loved him at the first did not forsake him; for he appeared to them alive again the third day; as the divine prophets had foretold these and ten thousand other wonderful things concerning him. And the tribe of Christians so named

58

from him, are not extinct at this day.''—Book 18, Chapter 3.

This eminent historian lived about 37 A. D. to about 100 A. D. Thus he had ample opportunity to investigate the claims that were made relative to Christ. He was not a Christian and, therefore, was not trying to establish the claims of Christianity; he was a historian and was only recording history as he found it. Josephus says that Christ lived; that he was a ''wise man if it be lawful to call him a man''; that he was a doer of wonderful works; that Pilate condemned him to the cross; that he arose the third day and appeared to his disciples. Thus the writings of an ancient, unchristian historian confirm the New Testament.

The credibility of the Bible is also corroborated by other ancient historians: Gaius Cornelius Tacticus, born about the middle of the first century and died in 117; Pliny, ''The Younger,'' 62 A. D. ? — 114 A. D. ?

11. We believe the Bible to be inspired of God because *no man can improve it*. All human works can be improved. Think of the improvements that have been made in science, industry, education and in every field. Old books are discarded for improved ones. But a book that was completed about nineteen hundred years ago continues to be the world's best seller. It graces almost every home and its words are on the lips of millions. ''Tradition has dug for it a grave, intolerance has lighted for it many a fagot, many a Judas has betrayed it with a kiss, many a Peter has denied it with an oath, many a Demas has forsaken it; but the word of God still endures.'' No man has been able to improve it or give us a better Bible. Is this not strange? Not at all! It was written by the Divine-Writer.

REASON X
BECAUSE IT BELIEVES THE BIBLE IS A BOOK TO BE RIGHTLY DIVIDED

I. INTRODUCTION

PAUL enjoined upon Timothy the command to rightly divide the Bible: "Give diligence to present thyself approved unto God, a workman that needeth not to be ashamed, handling aright the word of truth" (II Tim. 2:15). Many teachers and preachers have no such conception of the Bible. They do not know that man is to give diligence to rightly divide heaven's message. They are just as apt to take you to Psalms to learn of conversion as to the Acts of Apostles.

II. A DIVISION OF THE BOOKS

1. *A proper classification* of the books makes Bible study easier. The Old Testament is composed of thirty-nine books and the New contains twenty-seven.

2. In the Old Testament we find *books of law, history, poetry and prophecy.* The first five books of the Bible have been called law, because they contain the law of Moses. The next twelve books are classed as history. And there are six poetical books: Job, Psalms, Proverbs, Ecclesiastes, Song of Solomon and Lamentations. The other sixteen books of the Old Testament are classed as prophecy. Of course these classifications are not exclusive to other themes.

3. In the New Testament we have the *gospels, history of conversions, letters and prophecy.* The first four books are called the gospels. Acts of Apostles is known as the history of conversions. The next twenty-one books are letters to churches and Christians. Revelation is classified as prophecy.

III. A DIVISION OF THE DISPENSATIONS

A proper division of the dispensations is indispensable. They are three in number, namely: Patriarchal, Jewish and Christian.

1. *Patriarchal Dispensation:*

(1) The patriarchal has derived its name from the father of the family or tribe. Patriarch means father. Under this system the patriarch was prophet, priest and ruler. He directed the affairs of the family both religiously and politically. God spoke to the head of the family, and he, in turn, spoke to the members of the family.

(2) This has been called a family system of religion, as each family seems to have been left free under the guidance of God to carry on its own affairs. What was a command unto one patriarch may not have been a law unto the other patriarchs. For instance, God commanded Noah to build an ark, but the other patriarchs received no such command. Abraham was commanded to make preparations to slay his son, Isaac, but the command was not applicable to the heads of other families.

(3) They had no written system of religion. God spoke to the head of the tribe orally.

(4) This system of religion lasted for approximately twenty-five hundred years, from Adam to the giving of the law of Moses at Mt. Sinai; and it seems that it did not

terminate then, but was afterwards applicable only to the Gentiles.

2. *Jewish Dispensation:*

(1) This system grew out of the promise of the temporal and earthly blessing made to Abraham: "I will make of thee a great nation, and I will bless thee, and make thy name great; and be thou a blessing" (Gen. 12:2). The law was an outgrowth of the promise, and was given four hundred and thirty years after the promise was made (Gal. 3:16,17). That the promise might be kept, God gave them a government, the law of Moses, which guided them religiously and politically.

(2) The Jewish or Mosaic system was man's first written system of religion. Abraham's descendants, in their exodus from Egypt, were led to the foot of Mt. Sinai, and God gave to them the ten commandments written upon two tables of stone (Ex. 19, 20). Since then, man has had a "book" religion.

(3) The family system of worship was enlarged and developed into a national system. The tribe attended to the administration of government rather than have each father for a ruler or king. The same was true of the priesthood: One tribe devoted its time to the office of priesthood. They had one national altar and one national house of God.

(4) One purpose of the Jewish dispensation was to keep Abraham's posterity a separate and distinct race until the promised seed (Christ) should come (Gal. 3:16-19) This characteristic exclusiveness of the Mosaic dispensation has been called "the middle wall of partition," for it separated the Jews from other nations (Eph. 2:14).

(5) Another function of the law was to be "a shadow of the good things to come" (Heb. 10:1). The Lord used this system to picture in types and figures the more glorious system which was to come. Paul says, "Now these things happened unto them by way of example; and they were written for our admonition" (I Cor. 10:11). The wanderings in the wilderness were symbolic of God's people under the New Testament. The tabernacle and the temple were types of the church under this dispensation. The sacrificial lamb under the law was but typical of the Christ, the Lamb of God, who was to die for the sins of the world. Hagar, Ishmael, Sarah and Isaac are used by Paul to illustrate the two systems. Moses was a type of Christ who was to come. Surely, he who would understand the Christian religion must understand the law of Moses.

(6) Another object of the law was to be a schoolmaster or tutor, by which man could be brought to Christ (Gal. 3:24). The world was not prepared to receive Christ and his gospel. This schoolmaster was to train and educate men and bring them to Christ. By allowing the first covenant to tutor us, we are prepared for the second.

(7) The law was faulty: "For if that first covenant had been found faultless, then would no place have been sought for the second" (Heb. 8:7). Paul also declares that the law is weak: "For what the law could not do, in that it was weak through the flesh, God, sending his own Son in the likeness of sinful flesh and for sin, condemned sin in the flesh" (Rom. 8:3). One evident weakness was no complete forgiveness of sins and transgressions. All of the many sacrifices offered continually upon the altar of God resulted only in the moving forward of sins year by year and their ever being conscious of sin; "for it is impossible

that the blood of bulls and goats should take away sins" (Heb. 10:1-4).

(8) God intended for the Jewish dispensation to be temporary. It was to last only "till the seed should come to whom the promise hath been made" (Gal. 3:19). We are not left to guess as to the identity of the seed, for Paul said, "And to thy seed, which is Christ" (Gal. 3:16). Thus, the law was to be terminated by the Christ.

3. *Christian Dispensation*:

(1) This dispensation grew out of the spiritual promise made to Abraham: "And in thee shall all the families of the earth be blessed" (Gen. 12:3). We find a renewal of the promise in these words: "In thy seed shall all the nations of the earth be blessed" (Gen. 22:18). All the families and all the nations of the earth were to be blessed by a descendant of Abraham. That one was Christ who died for us and became the mediator of a better covenant.

(2) This is the new covenant of which Jeremiah prophesied: "Behold, the days come, saith Jehovah, that I will make a new covenant with the house of Israel, and with the house of Judah: not according to the covenant that I made with their fathers in the day that I took them by the hand to bring them out of the land of Egypt; which my covenant they brake, although I was a husband unto them, saith Jehovah. But this is the covenant that I will make with the house of Israel after those days, saith Jehovah: I will put my law in their inward parts, and in their heart will I write it; and I will be their God, and they shall be my people" (Jer. 31:31-33). Paul declares that this prophecy of the new covenant has been fulfilled (Heb. 8:6-13). God has, therefore, given us a new covenant and we are living under it today.

(3) The change of priesthoods necessitated the change of laws: "For the priesthood being changed, there is made of necessity a change also of the law" (Heb. 7:12). Jesus Christ is the high priest under the new priesthood (Heb. 9:11), and every child of God is a priest (I Pet. 2:5). The priesthood being changed, the law had to be changed. Hence, we are living under a law different from the one given to the Jews.

(4) Christ came to take "away the first, that he may establish the second" (Heb. 10:9). This was one of his objects in coming. The second has been established; therefore, the first has been taken away.

(5) Christ took away the law by nailing it to the cross: "Having blotted out the bond written in ordinances that was against us, which was contrary to us; and he hath taken it out of the way, nailing it to the cross" (Col. 2:14). Christ was born under the law (Gal. 4:4,5), lived under the law, and finally died under the law to fulfill it (Matt. 5:17). Christ lived and died under the Old Covenant. The things that transpired before his death were before the New Covenant became effective.

(6) The New Testament could not become operative until after the death of Christ: "For where a testament is, there must of necessity be the death of him that made it. For a testament is of force where there hath been death: for it doth never avail while he that made it liveth" (Heb. 9:16,17). We understand this for we see it demonstrated constantly. We know that no will or testament can become effective until after the testator has died. Paul declares the same concerning the testament of our Saviour. Christ's death on the cross fulfilled and ended the law (Col. 2:14),

and it was afterwards that the Christian dispensation became operative.

(7) The Christian dispensation has been given to all nations: "Go ye, therefore, and make disciples of all the nations" (Matt. 28:19). "Go ye into all the world, and preach the gospel to the whole creation" (Mk. 16:15). The middle wall of partition which stood between Jew and Gentile has been broken down (Eph. 2:14). Both may now be reconciled unto God in one body (Eph. 2:16), which is the church. Therefore, "There can be neither Jew nor Greek, there can be neither bond nor free, there can be no male and female; for ye are all one man in Christ Jesus" (Gal. 3:28).

(8) Today under the Christian dispensation, we must obey Christ. Moses prophesied: "Jehovah thy God will raise up unto thee a prophet from the midst of thee, of thy brethren, like unto me; unto him ye shall hearken" (Deut. 18:15). Peter teaches that this prophecy has been fulfilled, and "that every soul that shall not hearken to that prophet, shall be utterly destroyed from among the people" (Acts 3:22,23). This was reaffirmed at the transfiguration. Christ was transfigured, and Moses and Elijah also appeared. Peter wanted to build three tabernacles, one for each. But the plan was destroyed by these words of God: "This is my beloved Son, in whom I am well-pleased; hear ye him" (Matt. 17:5). There was a time when man was to listen to Moses and Elijah, but now he must listen to God's Son. Paul declares, "God, having of old time spoken unto the fathers in the prophets by divers portions and in divers manners, hath at the end of these days spoken unto us in his Son" (Heb. 1:1,2).

IV. A COMPARISON OF THE TWO COVENANTS

The First (Heb. 10:9)
1. Old Covenant (II Cor. 3:14).
2. Takes away first (Heb.10:9.
3. Given by prophets (Heb. 1:1,2).
4. Given to Jews (Gen. 17:13).
5. Written on stones (II Cor. 3:7).
6. Shadow of good things (Heb. 10:1).
7. Offering oftentimes the same sacrifices (Heb. 10:11).
8. Blood of animals (Heb. 10:1-4).
9. Animals as dead sacrifices (Heb. 10:1-4).
10. A remembrance of sins (Heb. 10:3).
11. Made nothing perfect or complete (Heb. 7:19).
12. Fleshly circumcision (Gen. 17:9-11).
13. Ministration of condemnation (II Cor. 3:9).
14. Levitical priesthood (Heb. 7:11).
15. Old priesthood and law (Heb. 7:12).
16. Faulty (Heb. 8:7).
17. Blotted out (Col. 2:14).

The Second (Heb. 10:9)
1. New Covenant (II Cor. 3:6).
2. Establishes second (Heb. 10:9).
3. Given by Christ (Heb. 1:1,2).
4. Given to every creature (Mk. 16:15,16).
5. Written in hearts (II Cor. 3:3).
6. The true (Heb. 8:1,2).
7. Christ offered once for all (Heb. 7:27).
8. Blood of Christ (Heb. 9:14).
9. Human body as living sacrifice (Rom. 12:1).
10. Sins remembered no more (Heb. 8:12).
11. Perfect or complete in Christ (Col. 1:28).
12. Circumcision of the heart (Rom. 2:29).
13. Ministration of righteousness (II Cor. 3:9).
14. Each Christian a priest (I Pet. 2:5).
15. Priesthood and law changed (Heb. 7:12).
16. Perfect law (Jas. 1:25).
17. Remaineth (II Cor. 3:11).

V. THE THIEF ON THE CROSS

At this point we need to answer an oft-repeated question: "What about the thief on the cross? If baptism is essential to salvation, why wasn't the thief baptized?"

Friend, we dare not think that Christ contradicted himself and that he is in some dilemma. Yet, baptism is essential to salvation (Mk. 16:16; Acts 2:38; Acts 22:16; I Pet. 3:20,21). So, what about the thief?

1. Permit me to suggest in the first place that *it cannot be proved that the thief had not been baptized.* John the Baptist went through the country baptizing folk, and this man who turned out to be a thief could have been baptized the same as others (Lk. 7:29,30; 3:21).

2. In the second place, we see that *there is no contradiction in the teachings of Christ, because this was under the law of Moses.* The law of Moses had not been fulfilled at this time, for Jesus had not died on the cross; he was still living. No man had ever been commanded at this time to be baptized in the name of the Father and of the Son and of the Holy Spirit. The thief lived and died under a dispensaton different from the one man is under today (Col. 2:14).

Perhaps an example will help to clarify the thought: Texas was an independent nation for ten years, and then voluntarily became a part of the United States. Suppose that after this change was made a Texan refused to salute the American flag. He was arrested and put in jail. He angrily shouted, "I did not have to salute the American flag under the Texan government and I do not have to under the American government." He employed a lawyer. Now it would be a very unlearned lawyer who would argue in court that because a man did not have to salute the American flag under the Texan government, therefore, he did not have to salute it under the American government. It is likewise a very unlearned preacher who will argue that because the thief and others could be saved under the law of Moses without being baptized, therefore, men today under the Christian dispensation can be saved without being baptized.

3. In the third place, *there is no contradiction, because "the Son of man hath authority on earth to forgive sins"* (Lk. 5:24). When Christ walked and talked among men on earth, he could say to the blind, "Receive your sight"; to the deaf, "Hear"; to the sick, "Arise and take up thy bed"; and to the one guilty of sins, "Thy sins are forgiven." Christ had that authority on earth; that was before his will or testament became effective, for it did not become effective until after Christ's death. In proof of which, we quote Paul: "For where a testament is, there must of necessity be the death of him that made it. For a testament is of force where there hath been death: for it doth never avail while he that made it liveth" (Heb. 9:16,17). But ever since Christ died and ever since his will has become operative, it must be executed according to the provisions that are found in it. Woe unto the man who changes it!

REASON XI

BECAUSE IT IS UNDENOMINATIONAL

I. INTRODUCTION

THE church of Christ is an undenominational institution. When we say undenominational, we do not mean all-denominational. Some men who claim to be undenominational are in reality all-denominational. They are all-denominational in that they look with favor upon all denominations. The church of Christ is undenominational in that it is not a denomination and in that it stands opposed to denominationalism.

II. DENOMINATIONALISM CONTRADICTS THE BIBLE

It is evident that denominationalism is antipodal to the Bible. For instance, examine the following:

Denominationalism	VS. Undenominational Christianity
1. Many bodies or churches.	1. One body or church (Matt. 16:18; I Cor. 12:20).
2. Founded by men.	2. Founded by Christ (Matt. 16:18).
3. Human heads.	3. Christ the head (Eph. 1:22,-23).
4. Human creeds.	4. Bible as only creed (II Tim. 3:16,17).
5. Wear human names.	5. Glorify God in the name Christian (I Pet. 4:16).
6. Follow men.	6. Following men is condemned (I Cor. 1:10-13).
7. A multiplicity of churches unknown to the Bible.	7. Mentioned in the Bible (Rom. 16:16).
8. Membership in denominations is not essential to salvation.	8. Membership in Christ's church is essential to salvation (Eph. 5:23).

70

9. Preach many gospels.

10. Rewrite creeds every few years.
11. Many faiths.
12. Many baptisms.
13. Join churches.

14. Claim to be abiding in branches of the church.
15. Walk by different rules.

16. Thank God in their prayers for so many churches.
17. Claim doctrine is inconsequential.

9. If a man preach any other gospel, he is condemned (Gal. 1:8,9).
10. Bible remains the same (Matt. 24:35).
11. "One faith" (Eph. 4:5).
12. "One baptism" (Eph. 4:5).
13. God adds to "the church" (Acts 2:47).
14. Jesus said, "Abide in me," the true vine (Jno. 15:1-6).
15. Walk by the same rule (Phil. 3:16).
16. Jesus prayed for oneness (Jno. 17:20,21).
17. Take heed unto doctrine to save self and others (I Tim. 4:16).

The above is only a brief contrast. It could be increased manyfold. But this should be enough to convince the convincible that denominationalism contradicts the Bible.

III. THE RISE OF CATHOLICISM AND DENOMINATIONALISM

The Lord established his church a little more than nineteen hundred years ago. This sacred institution remained pure and uncorrupted for a time. Then the predicted apostasy began to be fulfilled (Acts 20:29,30; II Thess. 2:1-4; I Tim. 4:1-3). The commandments and inventions of men led to the gradual development of the Roman Catholic Church. At a later date men tried to reform the Catholic Church, but their efforts only resulted in the establishment of more man-made churches. Their efforts gave birth to denominationalism with its hundreds of contradictory doctrines. All historians know that denominationalism is the offspring of Catholicism. But the church founded by Jesus and the apostles in the first century was neither the Roman Catholic Church nor the Protestant Church, but was Christ's church, the true church. Members were neither Catholics nor Protestants, but were Christians.

IV. THE RESTORATION OF UNDENOMINATIONAL CHRISTIANITY

In the beginning of the nineteenth century men began to present to the world a new plea, one that has spread with amazing rapidity and is revolutionizing the religious world. At the turn of the century there were simultaneous widespread efforts in the United States to restore to the world New Testament Christianity. These men did not labor to reform any human church or to give to the world another human church, but they endeavored to restore the true church which had become lost to the multitudes because of the doctrines of Catholicism and denominationalism. The restorers made a plea for men to become members of Christ's church only and be nothing but Christians. They knew that if they did what men did in the first century, they would be only what men were in the first century. They knew the same seed would produce the same crop and the same church. (See the discussion under Topic IV, Reason III.)

We note the work of some of these men, as follows:

1. *James O'Kelly and others of North Carolina* left the Methodist Church on December 25, 1793, and for a time took the name "Republican Methodists." However, in 1801 they resolved to be known as "Christians" only, to acknowledge no head over the church but Christ, and to have no creed but the Bible.

2. *A physician, Dr. Abner Jones of Vermont,* a Baptist, preached that partyism and sectarian names and creeds should be abolished. In September, 1800, he established a church at Lyndon, Vermont. He later established one in Bradford, and, in 1803, one in Piermont, New Hampshire. Elias Smith, a Baptist preacher, joined Dr. Jones' movement and carried the whole church with him.

3. *Chester Bullard* severed his connections with the Methodists because he came to believe in immersion as the act of baptism. However, he refused immersion from the Baptists, not believing in them. Bullard was finally immersed by a friend, Landon Duncan, County Assessor. He preached the night after he was baptized, and finally established several churches in Virginia.

4. *The largest restoration movement was led by Barton W. Stone,* a prominent preacher of Kentucky. Stone was at first a Presbyterian preacher, but his preaching was so different from the creed, the Westminister Confession of Faith, that the synod at Lexington, Kentucky, excommunicated him and some others. They at first organized themselves into an independent presbytery, Springfield Presbytery. About a year later they perceived that such was unscriptural and renounced it. In doing this they drew up the famous document, "The Last Will and Testament of the Springfield Presbytery," June 25, 1804. Here are some statements from the will:

(1) "We will, that this body die, be dissolved and sink into union with the body of Christ at large"; (2) "We will, that our name of distinction, with its reverend title, be forgotten"; (3) "We will, that our power of making laws for the government of the church, executing them by delegated authority, forever cease"; (4) "We will, that the

73

Church of Christ resume her native right of internal government"; (5) "We will, that the people henceforth take the Bible as their only guide."

This ended the Springfield Presbytery, and the will is conclusive evidence that they did not establish a new denomination. They dissolved a denomination to be un-denominational. In a few years this group numbered into the thousands.

This occurred five years before Alexander Campbell came to America. This alone should silence the unlearned who have unknowingly charged that Alexander Campbell established the church of Christ.

5. *Thomas Campbell, a Presbyterian preacher,* came to America in 1807. The Presbyterians censored him for being too liberal, and he withdrew from this body. At a called meeting of those who held similar views, in an old farm house, Campbell spoke and concluded his address by urging them to adopt the following principle: *"Where the Scriptures speak, we speak; where the Scriptures are silent, we are silent."* The principle was accepted and was the beginning of another restoration movement. There were many fundamental truths they had not grasped, but this principle led them into those truths one by one. It was decided August 17, 1809, that they would officially unite themselves into a regular body, known as the "Christian Association of Washington."

6. *Alexander Campbell, son of Thomas Campbell,* arrived in America on September 29, 1809. He heartily endorsed the restoration movement. The principle, "Speak where the Bible speaks and be silent where the Bible is silent," slowly but surely broke their fetters of denominationalism. They were baptized June 12, 1812, by Elder

74

Luce, a Baptist preacher, upon the confession Philip had the eunuch to make, Acts 8. This was contrary to Baptist doctrine; hence, they did not become Baptists. However, in 1813 the Campbells and the Brush Run Church joined the Redstone Association, a Baptist association, upon the condition that they could preach anything in the Bible, irrespective of any creed on earth. But as the Campbells got nearer the truth they got further away from the Baptists. Consequently, their fellowship with the Baptists became unpleasant for both groups and was broken little by little.

In 1832 at Lexington, Kentucky, there was a fusion of the forces of the Campbells—about twelve thousand— with those of Barton W. Stone, which numbered about fifteen thousand. This work of fusion and union continued because the Bible was their only guide. By the year of 1835 the restoration movements were united in a common cause. It is impossible for several groups to be divided when they preach the Bible, the whole Bible, and nothing but the Bible. The fact that the world is so badly divided is proof that all are not preaching the Bible.

It is evident from history that Alexander Campbell was not the founder of any church. The movement to restore primitive Christianity to the world was under way before he ever came to America. He severed his connections with creed-bound, human churches to be a Christian only. He supported the restoration movement by preaching, writing and debating. With his extraordinary ability he put the plea before the people as no other restorer had done. This was all that was needed for it to grow. Members of human churches walked out by the scores to be undenominational Christians. Some sectarian preachers, however, more interested in partyism than truth, stigmatized the movement as Campbellism and called it the Campbellite Church, hoping to arouse prejudice against the plea.

It is only fair and just that we note the words of Alexander Campbell in reply to the question, *"What is Campbellism?"* Hear his answer:

"It is a nickname of reproach invented and adopted by those whose views, feelings, and desires are all sectarian; who cannot conceive of Christianity in any other light than an ism. These isms are now the real reproaches of those who adopt them, as they are the intended reproaches of those who originate and apply them. He that gives them when they are disclaimed, violates the express law of Christ. He speaks evil against his brother, and is accounted as a railer or reviler, and placed along with haters of God and those who have no lot in the kingdom of heaven. They who adopt them out of choice disown the Christ and insult him; for they give the honor which is due to him alone to the creature of the Devil; for all slander and detractions are of the creation of the Devil. If Christians were wholly cast into the mould of the Apostles' doctrine, they would feel themselves as much aggrieved and slandered in being called by any man's name, as they would in being called a thief, a fornicator, or a drunkard. . . . . I have always disclaimed everything sectarian; and if the people of the different sects slander me or any of those who prefer the scriptures to any human creed, and the kingdom of Jesus the Messiah, to any sect; I say, if they slander us with the names and epithets which we disavow, they must answer to him who judges righteously.

"But for ourselves we protest against the name, the precepts, the feelings of any sect or schism in Christendom."—*Christian Baptist,* pages 451, 452.

It is evident that the church of Christ is not "just another denomination." It is the church that existed nineteen centuries ago. Every member has been added to it by the Lord himself (Acts 2:47) and has stopped there so far as church affiliation is concerned. It is undenominational with an unsectarian plea, a plea for the world to return to the ancient gospel.

REASON XII

BECAUSE IT IS SCRIPTURAL IN DOING MISSION-ARY WORK

I. THE NEED OF PREACHING

THE church of Christ has been falsely accused of being anti-missionary because it has no missionary society or organization other than the local church. To refute that accusation, I submit the following:

1. *It is Christ's command that the gospel be preached.* He said, "Go ye into all the world, and preach the gospel to the whole creation. He that believeth and is baptized shall be saved; but he that disbelieveth shall be condemned" (Mk. 16:15,16). It is as needful to obey the first part of the great commission as it is to obey the latter part of it. Obedience to the latter part is dependent upon man's obedience to the first part: upon taking the gospel to those who know it not.

2. *It is impossible to have gospel fruit without first sowing the seed of the kingdom.* In the parable of the sower Jesus put the sowing of the seed before the production of fruit (Matt. 13:3-8; 18-23). This parable is evidence that preaching the gospel is indispensable to the growth of Christ's kingdom.

3. *There can be no production of faith apart from hearing the Word:* "So belief cometh of hearing, and hearing by the word of Christ." (Rom. 10:17). Hearing the word of Christ produces faith. That is one reason why we have the written Word: "Many other

78

signs therefore did Jesus in the presence of the disciples, which are not written in this book: but these are written, that ye may believe that Jesus is the Christ, the Son of God; and that believing ye may have life in his name" (Jno. 20:30,31). Satan knows that this is the way faith is produced: "Then cometh the devil, and taketh away the word from their heart, that they may not believe and be saved" (Lk. 8:12). The Corinthians believed through this means: "And many of the Corinthians hearing, believed, and were baptized" (Acts 18:8).

4. *Men cannot be drawn to God apart from being taught of him*: "No man can come to me, except the Father that sent me draw him: and I will raise him up in the last day. It is written in the prophets, And they shall all be taught of God. Every one that hath heard from the Father, and hath learned, cometh unto me" (Jno. 6:44,45). The Father draws sinners unto Christ, and it is done through the Word. Then how important it is that we sound it out!

5. *Jesus placed teaching first in the system of conversion*: "For this people's heart is waxed gross, and their ears are dull of hearing, and their eyes they have closed; lest haply they should perceive with their eyes, and hear with their ears, and understand with their heart, and should turn again, and I should heal them" (Matt. 13:15). In this quotation we have the following arrangement: (1) Teaching—"perceive with their eyes, and hear with their ears." (2) Understanding. (3) Turning or conversion. (4) Healing or forgiveness. No teaching, no understanding; no understanding, no conversion; no conversion, no healing or forgiveness. This should impress upon Christians their duty to take the gospel. Just in proportion as we fail

to do our duty in preaching the gospel to the lost we fail in making it possible for them to be saved.

6. *The Lord's word is the begetting power in the process of the new birth*: "Having been begotten again, not of corruptible seed, but of incorruptible, through the word of God, which liveth and abideth" (I Pet. 1:23). Just as there can be no physical birth without a father, neither can there be a new birth without the teaching of God's word.

7. *Where there is no preaching, there can be no salvation.* Paul emphasized this fact, saying, "Whosoever shall call upon the name of the Lord shall be saved. How then shall they call on him in whom they have not believed? and how shall they believe in him of whom they have not heard? and how shall they hear without a preacher?" (Rom. 10:13,14). Let us begin at the last of the passage and go back to the first: where there is no preaching, there can be no hearing; no hearing, no believing; no believing, no calling; no calling, no salvation. So it does not matter whether we begin at the first and go to the last or begin at the last and go back to the first, we arrive at the same conclusion, namely: the gospel must be preached for souls to be saved.

8. *The inconsistency of some sects* is seen in that they contend that God converts people through a direct operation of the Holy Spirit, but conduct evangelistic campaigns and support missionaries. If this were true, there would be no need to preach. Consistency demands that they stand back in silence and let God convert sinners that way. If I were of that conviction, I would dismiss the preacher. Why have a preacher to preach that souls may be converted, if they are converted through a direct opera-

tion of the Holy Spirit apart from the Word? "O consistency, thou art a jewel."

II. THE CHURCH—THE DIVINE MISSIONARY SOCIETY

Any missionary society larger or smaller than or different from the congregation is unscriptural. In the first century the local church or congregation was the only missionary society. This agency for the dissemination of the gospel was so successful that in just a few years Paul could write, "the gospel which ye heard, which was preached in all creation under heaven" (Col. 1:23). This was accomplished without the aid of modern means of travel, the printing press and the radio. When will men learn that they cannot create missionary societies and plans comparable to the simple plan revealed in the New Testament?

God has placed upon the local church the responsibility of preaching the gospel:

1. *The wisdom of God is to be made known through the church*: "To the intent that now unto the principalities and the powers in the heavenly places might be made known through the church the manifold wisdom of God" (Eph. 3:10). The church rather than some missionary society is the institution to make known the truth.

2. *The Holy Spirit has enjoined upon the church the work of upholding the truth*: "But if I tarry long, that thou mayest know how men ought to behave themselves in the house of God, which is the church of the living God, the pillar and ground of the truth" (I Tim. 3:15). The fact that God has appointed the church to be "the pillar and ground of the truth" eliminates all societies and human agencies.

3. *We are taught to glorify God in the church*: "Unto him be glory in the church and in Christ Jesus unto all generations for ever and ever" (Eph. 3:21). To attempt to glorify the Father in some other institution is disobedience and an insult to God, the Author of this command.

4. *Man is commanded to do all religious work in the name of the Lord Jesus*: "And whatsoever ye do, in word or in deed, do all in the name of the Lord Jesus" (Col. 3:17). To work in the name of the Lord Jesus is to work by his authority. His authority demands that Christians work through the congregation as the only missionary society to make known the gospel. To work through some human missionary society is a refusal to abide by his authority.

5. *The missionary society has no scriptural head, foundation, field or mission.* Christ is not its head, for he is the head of the church; Christ is not its foundation, because the fact that he is the Son of God is the foundation of the church; the world cannot be its field, for the world is the field of the church; preaching the gospel is not its mission, for this is the mission of the church. Therefore, the missionary society is an unnecessary organization, having an unscriptural head to direct it, an unscriptural foundation to support it, an unscriptural field in which to labor, and an unscriptural mission for its existence.

6. *Our human wisdom enables us to see the inefficiency of such an organization.* It is said that it takes about fifty per cent—some societies more and some less—of the money contributed to fuel the machinery of the missionary society. Such has given rise to the saying: "Here's a dollar for the missionary, and here's another dollar for the society to send

it to him.'' It is obvious that the society is a sponge, which absorbs much of the funds that could be used in supporting the missionary.

About five years ago the writer heard a United States Senator in a speech over the radio state that when he was in World War I a letter came to the Y. M. C. A. box, but was addressed to God. After much discussion the boys decided to open it. It went something like this:

Dear God:

I am just a private in Uncle Sam's army. I have a little farm back in America and it has a debt hanging over it. A $100.00 note will soon come due. I don't want to lose my place. I wish you would send me the $100.00, please.

Yours truly,
PRIVATE BLANK.

This letter found a tender spot in the hearts of the soldiers, and they decided to pass around the hat and take up a collection for him. They did and the amount collected was $90.00, $10.00 short of the desired amount. They gave the $90.00 to the Y. M. C. A., and said organization sent it to the unfortunate soldier.

It was not long until another letter made its way to the Y. M. C. A., addressed to God. The soldiers standing around wanted to open it, too. It read something like this:

Dear God:

You recall that I asked you for $100.00 not long ago. I am grateful from the depths of my

83

heart for the money you sent me. But I want to give you this little tip: the next time you send me anything don't send it through the Y. M. C. A.; them buggers took out ten dollars, for I only got ninety.

Yours truly,
PRIVATE BLANK.

This illustration aptly describes the missionary society, for it is admitted by all that much has to be taken out to support the society.

The Lord's plan eliminates practically all of this expense of getting the money to the missionary. Every attempt on the part of man to improve God's system has resulted in tragic failure. God's plans are as far above the plans of man as the heavens are above the earth. When will man ever learn this lesson?

III. COOPERATION OF CHURCHES

The churches in the first century were independent, but they cooperated in exercising their duties. There was cooperation without organization. Paul's inspired language teaches that a plurality of churches may send funds to support an evangelist: "And ye yourselves also know, ye Philippians, that in the beginning of the gospel, when I departed from Macedonia, no church had fellowship with me in the matter of giving and receiving but ye only; for even in Thessalonica ye sent once and again unto my need" (Phil. 4:15,16). Paul took wages from a plurality of churches. He wrote: "I robbed other churches, taking wages of them that I might minister unto you" (II Cor. 11:8). These passages prove that churches may cooperate in preaching the gospel. If a church is too weak to completely support a preacher in other fields, then two or three congregations should cooperate in the effort. This would be cooperation without creating an organization to do the work that God has given to the church. Any cooperation maintained by an organization other than the congregation is unscriptural.

The church of Christ believes in mission work because the Bible teaches it. It believes in doing it through the congregation for the same reason: the Bible teaches it.

REASON XIII
BECAUSE IT TEACHES THE KINGDOM HAS BEEN ESTABLISHED AND CHRIST IS NOW REIGNING

I. INTRODUCTION

THE future kingdom theory together with the literal reign of Christ upon the earth for a literal thousand years has disturbed many people The theory has invaded many of the denominations of the world and is publicly advocated by their preachers. I could never cast my lot with a church which is lending its support to such a wild theory conceived by the unrestrained fantasy of men. It is called premillennialism; the theory that at the second coming of Christ man's earthly state will not be terminated but that a new age or dispensation of one thousand literal years will be inaugurated, during which time Christ will reign on the earth in Jerusalem for a literal thousand years, over a world of people still living in the flesh. No doubt some things are hard to understand, but it is not hard to understand that this cannot possibly be true.

II. THE KINGDOM HAS BEEN ESTABLISHED

First, it cannot be true because the kingdom has already been established:

1. Daniel, in recalling Nebuchadnezzar's forgotten dream and in giving the interpretation of it, said, "And in the days of those kings shall the God of heaven set up a kingdom which shall never be destroyed. . . . . it shall stand forever" (Dan. 2:44). What kings? Kings of the Roman

Empire, according to the interpretation of the dream in the light of sacred and secular history. God's ever-standing and never-ending kingdom was to be established while the Romans ruled over man.

2. In the days of those kings John the Baptist came preaching, "Repent ye; for the kingdom of heaven is at hand" (Matt. 3:1,2).

3. After John had been put in prison Jesus preached, "The time is fulfilled and the kingdom of God is at hand" (Mk. 1:15).

4. Jesus later taught the disciples to pray for the coming of the kingdom: "Our Father who art in heaven, hallowed be thy name. Thy kingdom come" (Matt. 6:9,10).

5. Christ taught that the kingdom was to come during the lifetime of some of the then-living disciples: "There are some here of them that stand by, who shall in no wise taste death, till they see the kingdom of God come with power" (Mk. 9:1). Either the kingdom has been established or else there are some disciples living in the world today who are more than nineteen hundred years old. In comparison with them, Methuselah died in his youth at the tender age of nine hundred and sixty nine years.

6. In Matt. 18:3 the disciples had not yet entered the kingdom, for Jesus said, "Except ye turn, and become as little children, ye shall in no wise enter into the kingdom of heaven."

7. In sending out the seventy Jesus said, "The kingdom of God is come nigh unto you" (Lk. 10:9). It was soon to be established.

8. But at the supper its establishment was still future: "I shall not drink from henceforth of the fruit of the vine, until the kingdom of God shall come" (Lk. 22:18).

9. We now come to the exact date the kingdom was established. You recall that Jesus said in Mk. 9:1 the kingdom was to come with power; you recall further that this power was to come upon the apostles in Jerusalem (Lk. 24:49). This power did come on the apostles in Jerusalem on the Pentecost following the resurrection of Christ (Acts 2:1-4); therefore, the kingdom came on Pentecost. Peter had been given the keys to the kingdom (Matt. 16:19). Keys are a symbol of authority. Thus, Peter had been given the authority to open the door of the kingdom or preach the terms of admission into it. Peter exercised this authority on Pentecost (Acts 2) by preaching the terms of admission into the kingdom; he used the keys and opened wide the door of entrance into the kingdom and propped it back for that generation and for all generations to enter. Three thousand became citizens of the kingdom on that day by virtue of their obedience to the divine plan: "They then that received his word were baptized: and there were added unto them in that day about three thousand souls" (Acts 2:41).

10. Paul, a few years after Pentecost, wrote that they had been translated into the kingdom: "Who delivered us out of the power of darkness and translated us into the kingdom of the Son of his love" (Col. 1:13). They could not have been translated into the kingdom, if it did not exist. The future kingdom theory flatly contradicts Paul.

11. The absurdity of the theory is again seen when placed along side of Heb. 12:28. "Wherefore, receiving a kingdom that cannot be shaken. . . . . " We have received a kingdom which cannot be shaken. If it cannot be shaken, then it will stand forever. If we have received a kingdom which will stand forever, then it cannot end to let another

begin. Hence, no kingdom can be established in the future.
12. It is preposterous to look for a kingdom to be established upon the earth. The kingdom has been established, and it is a spiritual rather than an earthly kingdom: "My kingdom is not of this world" (Jno. 18:36). It is to be regretted that man has devised a theory which positively denies these words of Jesus.

III. CHRIST'S THRONE IS IN HEAVEN

Second, premillennialism is unscriptural because Christ's throne is in heaven:

1. Zechariah said that Christ "shall sit and rule upon his throne" (Zech. 6:13). Christ is now sitting at God's right hand (Acts 2:30-35). Therefore, Christ's throne is at God's right hand. Not on the earth!

2. Zechariah declared that Christ would be a priest on his throne (Zech. 6:13). Paul said that Christ is a great high priest in heaven (Heb. 4:14). Therefore, Christ's throne is in heaven. Not on the earth!

3. Wherever Christ cannot be a priest he cannot have his throne, for Christ "shall be a priest on his throne" (Zech. 6:13). Christ cannot be a priest on earth: "For if he were on earth, he would not be a priest" (Heb. 8:4). Therefore, it is impossible for his throne to be on earth. It must be in heaven!

IV. CHRIST IS ON DAVID'S THRONE

Third, the fact that Christ is now on David's throne indicts the theory as being fanciful:

1. God promised that he would give Christ the throne of David (Lk. 1:32). This promise has been fulfilled: "Being therefore a prophet, and knowing that God had sworn with an oath to him, that of the fruit of his loins he would

set one upon his throne; he foreseeing this spake of the resurrection of the Christ" (Acts 2:30,31). Christ was resurrected to sit on the throne of David; therefore, he is now on David's throne. To say that he is not is a denial of his resurrection.

2. Zechariah informs us that Christ was to "sit and rule upon his throne" (Zech. 6:13). The sitting and ruling would be contemporaneous and simultaneous. When Christ began sitting he began ruling and vice versa. If we can prove that he is now sitting, we shall have proved that he is now ruling. Hear the proof: "This Jesus did God raise up, whereof we all are witnesses. Being therefore by the right hand of God exalted, and having received of the Father the promise of the Holy Spirit, he hath poured forth this, which ye see and hear. For David ascended not into the heavens; but he saith himself, The Lord said unto my Lord, sit thou on my right hand, till I make thine enemies the footstool of thy feet" (Acts 2:32-35). Christ is now sitting at the right hand of God; therefore, he is now ruling on his throne.

V. THE LAST DAYS

Fourth, the theory is untrue because it teaches we are not living in the last days. Peter's statement on the day of Pentecost, "This is the last days," is sufficient to prove the theory rdiculously false. All premillennialists hold that we are not living in the last days. They teach that Christ will inaugurate a period of days lasting one thousand years at his coming. But Peter said, "This is that which hath been spoken through the prophet Joel: and it shall be in the last days" (Acts 2:16,17). Peter says this, the day of Pentecost, the day the kingdom was established was the last days. Hence, when these days are over there will not

90

be any more days; then there will be the everlasting day. Another time the premillennialists are at variance with the Holy Spirit!

VI. I COR. 15:23-25

Fifth, the fallacy of premillennialism is again clearly seen when placed beside I Cor. 15:23-25. As we read this passage I shall insert a few words in brackets for emphasis' sake: "But each in his own order: Christ the firstfruits; then they that are Christ's at his coming [the resurrection at the coming of Christ]. Then cometh the end [not the beginning of a thousand years], when he shall deliver up the kingdom to God, even the Father [not establish it]; when he shall have abolished all rule and all authority and power [not that he is going to begin to rule]. For he must reign till he hath put all enemies under his feet" [not begin to reign, but reign now and continue to reign till the end]. This one passage proves the theory to be at variance with the Bible on many points.

VII. THE EARTH WILL BURN UP

Sixth, Christ will not reign upon this earth when he comes, because at that time the earth will burn up: "But the day of the Lord will come as a thief; in the which the heavens shall pass away with a great noise, and the elements shall be dissolved with fervent heat, and the earth and the works that are therein shall be burned up" (II Pet. 3:10). Where are the future-kingdom theorists going to have Christ's kingdom and put his throne? Not on the earth! For it will melt with fervent heat!

VIII. REV. 20:1-6 DOES NOT PROVE PREMILLENNIALISM

1. *Premillennialists' number-one text is Rev.* 20:1-6, *but it does not prove their contention:* The fact that Revela-

tion is a book of symbols and figures of speech makes it all the more difficult to explain. But notice that which the passage does not mention which is necessary to prove the premillennial contention: (1) The second coming of Christ. (2) Christ's reign on earth. (3) A resurrection of the body. (4) Does not mention Christ's ever being on this earth again. (5) Does not say that we shall reign with him —says, "They [the ones beheaded for the testimony of Jesus] lived and reigned with him a thousand years."

2. *The passage is teeming with figurative language,* as follows: "the key of the abyss," "chain in his hand," "shut it and sealed it," "thrones," "saw the souls," "the beast," "his image," "the mark upon their forehead and upon their hand," "first resurrection," "second death," "reign with him a thousand years." The premillennialists have chosen a passage that abounds with symbols—they admit it—and from it have picked out the phrase, "reign with him a thousand years," and insist that it be taken literally, even though it opposes plain statements which teach otherwise. Suppose they tell us why the thousand years should be taken literally while other phrases in the passage should be taken figuratively.

3. *Concerning the passage, Adam Clarke has said* in his commentary, "How many visions have been seen on this subject, both in ancient and modern times! This, and what is said in verses 3, 4, and 5 no doubt refer to a time in which the influence of Satan will be greatly restrained, and the true church of God enjoy great prosperity, which will endure for a long time. But it is not likely that the number, a thousand years, is to be taken literally here. . . . . It may signify that there shall be a long and undisturbed state of Christianity; and so universally shall the Gospel

spirit prevail, that it will appear as if Christ reigned upon earth; which will in effect be the case, because his spirit shall rule in the hearts of men; and in this time the martyrs are represented as living again; their testimony being revived, and the truth for which they died, and which was confirmed by their blood, being now everywhere prevalent. As to the term thousand years, it is a mystic number among the Jews.'' Inasmuch as the language is symbolic, Adam Clarke wrote, ''It may signify . . . . .''; he was not certain. Quite a contrast in his reserved language and the premillennialists' effusive speech!

Space would not permit as much material to go into this chapter as the author desired; so he recommends to the studious a volume devoted wholly to the study of this topic, one to which he is indebted for some of the material found in this chapter: Neal-Wallace Discussion On The Thousand Years Reign of Christ, published by the Gospel Advocate Co., Nashville, Tennessee.

REASON XIV

BECAUSE IT GIVES SCRIPTURAL ANSWERS TO THE QUESTION—WHAT MUST I DO TO BE SAVED?

I. THE QUESTION ANALYZED

WHAT." This word suggests that there is something required of man in being saved. He who asks the question understands this fact.

2. "*Must.*" This word indicates that it is not a question of what "should" I, or what "may" I, but what "must" I do? It is not a matter of option. The word "must" teaches the absolute necessity of the requirement.

3. "*I.*" It is not what God, Christ and the Holy Spirit must do, but what must "I" do. All know that the Trinity has a part in man's salvation. God, Christ and the Holy Spirit have perfectly executed the divine part in man's salvation. But the inquirer is not seeking to learn the functions of the Trinity. The "I" in the question denotes individual responsibility in human redemption.

4. "*Do.*" It is not what I must get, think, feel or believe. The word "do" suggests activity on the part of man in being saved. Salvation is not a matter of passiveness, but of activity. God saves; still, man saves himself by obeying the gospel, God's power to save (Rom. 1:16; Acts 2:40). Take the word "do" out of Christianity and you destroy it. You never read of an inspired man's telling a sinner that there is nothing for him to do to be saved.

5. "*To be saved.*" This phrase denotes the purpose of complying with the conditions. "To be saved" is the object

sought by the querist. The phrase also suggests that the saving is done by another. But what must man do to be saved by the Heavenly Father?

II. A SURE WAY TO ANSWER THE QUESTION

1. There could be no plainer, wiser and surer way to answer the question than to *turn to the Bible and read the question and the answer given.* If the question is found one hundred times, then read each question and each answer given thereto. This would be scriptural and right beyond question; furthermore, it would present the whole truth on the subject. But we do not find the question a hundred times. We find it, substantially, only four times in the New Testament, and one of these was under the law of Moses.

2. *The question was first propounded by the rich young man who came to Jesus* (Mk. 10:17). Jesus referred him to the ten commandments. The Mosaic law was in force at this time, for Christ had not yet died and nailed it to the cross (Col. 2:14). It was a Jew's duty to keep it. When the young man replied that he had kept the law from his youth, Jesus said, "One thing thou lackest; go, sell whatsoever thou hast, and give to the poor, and thou shalt have treasure in heaven: and come, follow me." The law of Moses had not been abrogated and he was to keep it; also, he needed to free himself of his riches which were a stumbling block to him; in addition, he was directed to follow Christ, as the disciples did, and he would be better trained for work in the coming dispensation. This answer would not be given today, because it was before the New Testament had become effective (Heb. 9:16,17).

95

It is good for us to observe that this Jew "went away sorrowful; for he was one that had great possessions." He seemed to be sincere in asking what to do, but he did not want to know. He only intended to obey, if it pleased him. Tragically, many are like that today. There are legions who think they want to be saved, but in reality do not.

3. *The question has been recorded three times in Acts.* Strangely enough, three different answers were given. Each answer was given by the authority of the Holy Spirit. All must be done. Let us study each and see the harmony in these seemingly contradictory answers.

III. THE JEWS ON PENTECOST

1. *The question and its answer.* In Acts 2 we read of the coming of the Holy Spirit upon the apostles. The object of this was to guide and direct them into the preaching of the gospel. Jews from every nation were dwelling there. When each heard in his own tongue, the excitement ran high. Some marveled, but others made light of what they had heard and tried to pass it off by accusing the apostles of being "filled with new wine." Peter's sermon followed this accusation. The preaching of God's word pricked their hearts and they asked, "Brethren, what shall we do" (Acts 2:37)? Peter replied: "Repent ye, and be baptized every one of you in the name of Jesus Christ unto the remission of your sins; and ye shall receive the gift of the Holy Spirit" (Acts 2:38). Why were they not told to believe? Because they had believed: so much so that they wanted to know what to do to be saved. Peter told these believers to repent and be baptized unto the remission of sins. According to Peter, baptism is just as essential as repentance. Both are coupled together by the copulative conjunction

"and" and point to the same object, the remission of sins. If repentance is unto the remission of sins, so is baptism.

2. *Salvation requires more than faith and a change of heart.* Not only had the Jerusalem inquirers believed, but they had experienced a change of heart. At the beginning of the event they accused the apostles of being intoxicated. Later, after hearing the gospel, they wanted to know what to do to be saved. They had believed and had experienced a change of heart, but were not saved. We are sure of this, because Peter did not say, as some preachers are saying, "All you have to do to be saved is just believe and have a change of heart." No! Peter told them to repent and be baptized unto the remission of sins. They believed; they had a change of heart, in a measure; but, in addition to this, they had to repent and be baptized in order for their sins to be remitted.

IV. SAUL OF TARSUS

1. *Saul, later known as Paul, is introduced as a persecutor.* He is first mentioned in connection with the stoning of Stephen (Acts 7:58,8:1). He later spoke of himself, by saying "as touching zeal, persecuting the church" (Phil. 3:6). He was exceedingly bitter in trying to stop the mouths of Christians (Acts 26:10,11). Even though he was an unsparing persecutor, his conscience was clear. He could say, "Brethren, I have lived before God in all good conscience until this day" (Acts 23:1). His conscience did not hurt, because he thought he was doing the right thing (Acts 26:9). This is certain proof that man's conscience cannot be accepted as the guide in religious matters. As long as a man thinks he is right, his conscience is clear. Saul had a good conscience, thinking

he was right; but he was wrong. This is true of many good people today.

2. *Saul's question and the answer given.* As Saul journeyed on the road to Damascus to persecute Christians, a light shone round about him and he heard the voice of Jesus. Jesus did not appear to Saul to pardon him, as some think, but to make him a "minister and a witness" (Acts 26:16). This miraculous event did not save him. After asking what to do, Jesus replied, "Rise and enter into the city, and it shall be told thee what thou must do" (Acts 9:6). Obviously, there is something to do. Saul lacked something. It was not faith; he had believed. Neither was it repentance; he was so penitent that he spent three days fasting and praying (Acts 9:9,11), while waiting to be told what he must do. Nor did he lack a change of heart; his heart had changed from a desire to persecute Christians to a desire to become a Christian. He lacked something, but it was not faith, repentance or a change of heart. No one has ever shown greater evidence of these than Saul. Was he saved? No! His sins had not been washed away. Christ said that he would be told what he must do. What was it? Ananias came to him and said, "And now why tarriest thou? arise, and be baptized, and wash away thy sins, calling on his name" (Acts 22:16). This is the second answer to the question. It is plain that men are wrong in thinking that faith, repentance and a change of heart are all that God has required of man to be saved.

V. THE JAILOR

Paul and Silas were prisoners in the Philippian jail. About midnight there was an earthquake. "All the doors were opened; and every one's bands were loosed." The jailor was "roused out of sleep." Seeing the prison doors open, thinking the prisoners had fled, he "drew his sword and was about to kill himself." But Paul stayed his hand. The jailor, trembling with fear, "fell down before Paul and Silas, and brought them out and said, Sirs, what must I do to be saved?" (Acts 16:30). This querist was an unbeliever. There is no evidence that he had ever heard a gospel sermon. They told him to "believe on the Lord Jesus and thou shalt be saved, thou and thy house" (Acts 16:31). But the story does not end here: "And they spake the word of the Lord unto him" (Acts 16:32). Why? So that he could believe (Rom. 10:17). The jailor then repented ("washed their stripes") "and was baptized, he and all his, immediately" (Acts 16:33). Saul had been told to be baptized in order to wash away his sins. Surely, he told the jailor to be baptized for the same reason. "God is no respecter of persons" (Acts 10:34).

VI. THREE DIFFERENT ANSWERS TO THE SAME QUESTION

We have read three different answers to the same question. The explanation is not hard:

1. *The jailor was an unbeliever.* He was told to believe. They preached to him for the purpose of producing faith. He then repented and was baptized.

2. *The people on Pentecost did believe.* So they were told to repent and be baptized for the remission of sins.

3. *Saul was a believing, penitent man.* He was told to be baptized and wash away his sins.

4. They were given different answers, because *they were at different places on the road to salvation.* But all did the same things and traveled over the same road. For

instance, a man asks how far it is from here to Dallas. He is told thirty miles. He drives up the way ten miles and asks again. This time, he is told twenty miles. The traveler drives up the road ten miles farther and asks again the same question. The answer is again different. He is now told ten miles. He was given three different answers to the same question. The same is true of the question, "What must I do to be saved?" The unbeliever had not begun to travel the road to pardon. He was told to believe; and, after believing, he repented and was baptized. The believers were not told to believe, but to repent and be baptized. Saul, the penitent believer, was not told to believe and repent; he was told to be baptized and wash away his sins. All traveled over the same road. All were converted alike. The Bible does not contradict itself. In answering the question scripturally, man must give all three answers that were given by the Holy Spirit. Man can no more change, by divine authority, this law of God than he can black out the sun, change the wind, or stop the snows.

REASON XV

BECAUSE IT TEACHES THAT MAN IS SAVED BY FAITH BUT NOT BY FAITH ONLY

I. WHAT IS FAITH

FAITH *is believing something as a result of testimony or evidence.* The Bible is a book of testimony, given to create faith in the human heart, for "these are written that ye may believe" (Jno. 20:30,31). People who have not this revelation know nothing of Christ. Where there is no testimony or evidence there can be no faith.

2. In a broader sense, *"faith is assurance of things hoped for, a conviction of things not seen"* (Heb. 11:1). Faith is the assurance or foundation of things hoped for. It is the support of all our hopes. "The assurance of things hoped for" means the assurance that they do exist. I have never seen London, Paris or Mexico City, but I have the assurance that they are in existence. I have never seen Christ in person, but I have the assurance that he died and "ever liveth."

II. HOW FAITH IS ACQUIRED

Many good people contend that faith comes as a result of a miraculous operation upon the human heart. If this were true, all men would believe; for "God is no respecter of persons" (Acts 10:34). Thus the development of faith cannot be ascribed to a falling agency from the heavens which hits some and misses others. Faith comes to rational people through rational means, as we shall see:

101

1. *The divine record was given to produce faith*: "These are written that ye may believe that Jesus is the Christ" (Jno. 20:31).

2. Christ's prayer teaches that *we believe on him through the words of the apostles*: "Neither for these only do I pray, but for them also that believe on me through their word" (Jno. 17:20).

3. Paul states that *faith or belief comes through the word of Christ*: "So belief cometh of hearing, and hearing by the word of Christ" (Rom. 10:17).

4. Peter says that *faith is dependent upon hearing*: "Brethren, ye know that a good while ago God made choice among you, and that by my mouth the Gentiles should hear the word of the gospel, and believe" (Acts 15:7).

5. *In the conversion of the Corinthians, hearing the word was the faith-producing agent*: "And many of the Corinthians hearing believed, and were baptized" (Acts 18:8).

6. *That angels know the word of God produces faith* is evident from the record of the conversion of Cornelius: "He told us how he had seen the angel standing in his house, and saying, Send to Joppa, and fetch Simon, whose surname is Peter; who shall speak unto thee words, whereby thou shalt be saved, thou and all thy house" (Acts 11:13,14). The words would enable him to believe and thus be saved.

7. *The devil knows that God's word is the basis of faith;* for that reason, he labors to steal it from the heart: "Then cometh the devil, and taketh away the word from their heart, that they may not believe and be saved." (Lk. 8:12).

These passages clinch the thought. God, Christ, the

Holy Spirit, the apostles, angels, and the devil know that faith comes by the Word.

III. THE NECESSITY OF FAITH

The absolute necessity of faith is emphasized from the beginning to the end of the Bible. It is indispensable to man's salvation. A refusal to accept faith as a condition of salvation is but a refusal to accept the Bible, because:

1. Man's heart is cleansed by faith (Acts 15:9).

2. Man is justified by faith (Rom. 5:1).

3. Faith is necessary to salvation (Acts 16:31; Mk. 16:16).

4. "We walk by faith, not by sight" (II Cor. 5:7). In this life we walk by faith, but in heaven we shall walk by sight. We shall then see the things that are now invisible (II Cor. 4:16-18; 5:6-8).

5. The Christian life is lived in faith (Gal. 2:20).

6. "Without faith it is impossible to be well-pleasing unto" God (Heb. 11:6).

7. "Whatsoever is not of faith is sin" (Rom. 14:23). Every act of obedience and service in the Christian religion is based upon faith. To be guided by your opinions in the realm of religion is not acceptable unto God. There must be faith, or the act is wrong.

IV. THE DOCTRINE OF FAITH ONLY CONTRADICTS THE BIBLE

The above citations stress the importance of faith in God's plan. Unfortunately, men have added the word "only" to these passages in an effort to prove justification by faith only. The error is widespread, taught by a multiplicity of churches, and many honest folk have been misled. No one sees the need of faith any more than I, but to interpret the passages which mention faith to teach justification by faith only would be a flat contradiction of other plain passages. For instance:

1. James declares that *faith apart from works is dead*: "Even so faith, if it have not works, is dead in itself" (Jas. 2:17).

2. If the doctrine of "faith only" were true, *it would save demons;* for "the demons also believe, and shudder" (Jas. 2:19).

3. *"Faith only" is mentioned in the New Testament;* but instead of teaching justification by it, it teaches the very opposite: "Ye see that by works a man is justified, and not only by faith" (Jas. 2:24). "Not by faith only" (K.J.V.). Every person who teaches justification by faith only does violence to the Scriptures and denies the inspired message of James.

4. James illustrates the thought by saying that *faith apart from works is as dead as a corpse*: "For as the body apart from the spirit is dead, even so faith apart from works is dead" (Jas. 2:26). He who teaches salvation by faith only disseminates a doctrine as dead as a dead man. The words of James alone should forever silence the advocates of this doctrine.

5. *Many of the rulers believed, but they were not saved*: "Nevertheless even of the rulers many believed on him; but because of the Pharisees thy did not confess it, lest they should be put out of the synagogue: for they loved the glory that is of men more than the glory that is of God" (Jno. 12:42,43). They denied Christ. Their doom is certain: "But whosoever shall deny me before men, him

104

will I also deny before my Father who is in heaven" (Matt. 10:33). These rulers believed; nevertheless they were not saved. They denied our Lord because there was something they loved more than his glory. Many of the world's multitudes today are in the same plight. They believe, but they love the works of the flesh more than obedience.

V. SAVED BY FAITH WHEN FAITH OBEYS

Man is saved by faith: "Believe on the Lord Jesus, and thou shalt be saved." But when is man saved by faith? the moment he believes? or when faith obeys? We shall see:

1. *The walls of Jericho fell by faith*—not the moment the people believed, but *after they had complied with the divinely given conditions*: "By faith the walls of Jericho fell down, after they had been compassed about seven days" (Heb. 11:30). If some of the "faith only" advocates had been present to have honestly but blindly led the people into disobedience, saying, "You don't have to do anything but believe; just sit here and wait for the walls to fall," would they have fallen? No! That would not have been faith in God. Faith in God is believing what God says. He gave them conditions to meet (Joshua 6). To have done other than what God had specified would have been positive proof of a lack of faith. This was a test of their faith. They believed and the walls fell by faith, but when? "After they were compassed about seven days." Man may call it a marching religion or anything he pleases, but the fact remains that the walls did not fall by faith until that faith obeyed.

2. *By faith Noah and his house were saved* (Heb. 11:7)—*but when?* That is the question. Suppose Noah had been of the persuasion of a multitude of present-day

preachers, and had said, "Faith only will save. There is no need to build an ark. If I build it, it will appear that I think God cannot save me." Well, they would have been lost. It is not a matter of what God can do, but rather what God will do. God told Noah what to do to be saved, and "By faith Noah . . . . . prepared an ark to the saving of his house." He was saved by faith. But when? When faith obeyed!

3. In Num. 21 we read that the Israelites were bitten by fiery serpents. "Much people of Israel died." Moses prayed to God in behalf of the people. *The divinely given way of escape was dependent upon faith*: "Make thee a fiery serpent, and set it upon a standard: and it shall come to pass, that every one that is bitten, when he seeth it, shall live" (Num. 21:8). Words of salvation were spoken. Dying men could be saved. By faith only? No! By complying with the condition. *They were saved when faith obeyed.* If many of the religionists of this age had been present, they would have preached: "Just believe and you will be saved. You do not have to look at the brazen serpent. That is snake religion and snake salvation." They would have said this then because they now say: "Just believe and you will be saved. You do not have to be baptized. That is water religion and water salvation." Looking at the brazen serpent was not snake salvation; it was salvation by faith. Neither is baptism water salvation; it is salvation by faith. There is no controversy about salvation by faith. The question is, "When is one saved by faith?" When faith complies with the conditions!

VI. JUSTIFICATION ASCRIBED TO SEVERAL AGENTS

The New Testament ascribes justification to several

106

agents or causes. We shall list some of these with the designation of each:

1. "Justified freely by his grace" (Rom. 3:24)— *God's grace, the motive agent.*

2. "By him [Christ] every one that believeth is justified" (Acts 13:39)—*Christ, the ready agent.*

3. "Justified by his blood" (Rom. 5:9)—*Christ's blood, the procurable agent.*

4. "Justified in the name of the Lord Jesus Christ" (I Cor. 6:11)—*the name or authority of the Lord, the immediate agent.*

5. "Justified by faith" (Rom. 5:1)—*man's faith, the human basic agent.*

6. "By works a man is justified" (Jas. 2:24)—*man's works, the human active agent.*

An example may help to clarify these facts: A gentleman hears the agonizing cries of a drowning man in his creek below the house. Moved purely by grace and good will, he sends his son to save the man. The son throws the perishing man a rope and invites him to grasp it and be saved. The drowning man seizes the rope and is saved. The motive agent in his salvation was the grace and good will of the father who heard the cries; the son was the ready agent; the act of throwing the rope was the procurable agent; the rope was the immediate agent; the drowning man's faith in the man on the bank and the rope was the human basic agent; catching hold of the rope was the human active agent. Thus the lost in sin are justified by grace, by Christ, by blood, by the name or authority of Christ, by faith and by works. When man assumes that faith is the only agent in man's salvation to the exclusion of all other agents, surely he has been misled. Faith is a part of the plan of salvation, but not the whole of it. Every agent in its own place is indispensable to man's justification.

REASON XVI

BECAUSE IT TEACHES THAT MAN IS SAVED BY THE BLOOD OF CHRIST

I. THE SIGNIFICANCE OF BLOOD IN THE DIVINE ECONOMY

IN all ages there has been efficacy and procuring power in blood. The sacrifice of blood has always been the sacrifice of life, "for the blood is the life" (Deut. 12:23). In each dispensation God has demanded a sacrifice of a bloody nature. This alone emphasizes the atoning power of blood; but we study further.

1. In the early dawn of time (Gen. 4) *Abel "brought of the firstlings of his flock" a sacrifice to Jehovah.* It was accepted. But Cain, his brother, "brought of the fruit of the ground an offering unto Jehovah." It was rejected. This first bloody sacrifice was a type of the blood of Christ shed for the sins of the world.

2. *Faithful Abraham, the friend of God, understood the importance of offering bloody sacrifices to God.* He hesitated not when commanded to offer Isaac, the child of promise, upon the altar. But as he took the knife to slay his son, the angel of Jehovah stayed his hand. A ram caught in the thicket was offered in Isaac's stead (Gen. 22:1-19).

3. *The institution of the Passover is further proof of the importance of blood in the divine economy.* When Jehovah went forth to deliver the Israelites and destroy their enemies, the Egyptians, the blood of lambs "upon the lintel, and on the two side-posts" was the token of safety and security. God had promised, "When I see the blood, I will

109

pass over you, and there shall no plague be upon you to destroy you, when I smite the land of Egypt" (Ex. 12:13). The children of Israel obeyed and there was not a single death among them. In this type we have a warning: Another day will come in which the messenger of destruction will go forth "in flaming fire, rendering vengeance to them that know not God, and to them that obey not the gospel of our Lord Jesus" (II Thess. 1:7,8). Just as the Israelites were spared by the blood of lambs, so those cleansed by the blood of Christ will be spared at the last day. What a joy it will be to stand among those who "washed their robes, and made them white in the blood of the Lamb."

4. *The sealing of the covenants with blood also bears testimony to the importance of blood in God's plan.* The children of Israel expressed a desire to keep the ordinances that Moses had received from God. Burnt-offerings and peace offerings went up unto Jehovah, and the blood of these animals was used to seal the covenant between God and man. We have a description of the ceremony in Ex. 24:6-8. The writer of Hebrews spoke of this ceremony in Heb. 9:19,20.

5. *Also, the tabernacle and all the vessels of the ministry were sanctified and sealed by the blood of animals:* "Moreover the tabernacle and all the vessels of the ministry he sprinkled in like manner with the blood. And according to the law, I may almost say, all things are cleansed with blood, and apart from shedding of blood there is no remission" (Heb. 9:21,22).

6. *The Jewish system was one in which animal sacrifices were offered in multiplied numbers, but they could not remove one sin:* "For the law having a shadow of the

good things to come, not the very image of the things, can never with the same sacrifices year by year, which they offer continually, make perfect them that draw nigh. Else would they not have ceased to be offered? because the worshippers, having been once cleansed, would have had no more consciousness of sins. But in those sacrifices there is a remembrance made of sins year by year. For it is impossible that the blood of bulls and goats should take away sins" (Heb. 10:1-4). "The same sacrifices year by year" were continually offered. But all the blood of animals shed on Israel's altars could not expiate one sin. Then, what was the purpose of such? It only moved forward the weight of sin for a year at a time. At the expiration of the time it became necessary to repeat the same act of sacrifice for another year. This was the procedure under the law of Moses. The blood of bulls and goats could not take away sins. But the Jews who faithfully offered the blood of animals unto God finally had all sins blotted out by the precious blood of Christ.

7. In Heb. 9, 10 *we have a clear and forceful analogy with reference to the blood of animals and the blood of Christ*: (1) The first covenant was dedicated by blood and likewise the new covenant was blood-sealed. (2) The Israelites had the weight of sin moved forward by the offering of sacrifices year by year, but we may actually be forgiven of sin by the blood of Christ. (3) The High Priest went into the Holy of Holies each year with blood, "which he offered for himself, and for the errors of the people"; however, Christ, our perfect High Priest, offered not the blood of animals for his sins, for he had none, but offered his own blood for man's sins and then with the merit of that blood ascended into heaven to appear before God for us.

111

8. *The conclusion is*: "Apart from shedding of blood there is no remission" (Heb. 9:22).

II. CHRIST'S BLOOD WAS SHED FOR HUMAN REDEMPTION

Nothing in the Bible is more clearly taught than the above caption. Reference was made to this fact in the preceding section, but it is not amiss to consider some more of the many passages teaching this blessed thought.

1. *Isaiah foresaw our being healed by Christ's stripes and wounds*: "But he was wounded for our transgressions, he was bruised for our iniquities; the chastisement of our peace was upon him; and with his stripes we are healed. All we like sheep have gone astray; we have turned every one to his own way; and Jehovah hath laid on him the iniquity of us all" (Isa. 53:5,6).

2. *Zechariah prophesied of the fountain opened for sin*: "In that day there shall be a fountain opened to the house of David and to the inhabitants of Jerusalem, for sin and for uncleanness" (Zech. 13:1). The prophecy has been fulfilled, and today we sing:

> There is a fountain filled with blood
> Drawn from Immanuel's veins;
> And sinners, plunged beneath that flood,
> Lose all their guilty stains.

3. *Christ, in instituting the Lord's supper,* said, "This is my blood of the covenant which is poured out for many unto remission of sins" (Matt. 26:28).

4. *One of the fundamental facts of the gospel* is "that Christ died for our sins according to the scriptures" (I Cor. 15:1-4).

5. *Hear the words of Paul in Rom.* 5:8 relative to the vicarious suffering of Christ: "But God commendeth his

own love toward us, in that, while we were yet sinners, Christ died for us.''

6. *The Gentiles,* ''alienated from the commonwealth of Israel, and strangers from the covenants of the promise, having no hope and without God in the world,'' being ''far off,'' *''are made nigh in the blood of Christ''* (Eph. 2:11-13).

7. *The blood was shed for every race, class, tongue and color, for every man on every shore and in every clime.* Jesus tasted ''of death for every man'' (Heb. 2:9). In John's Revelation we are told, ''For thou wast slain, and didst purchase unto God with thy blood men of every tribe, and tongue, and people, and nation'' (Rev. 5:9).

8. Peter declares that *ye were redeemed with the blood of Christ:* ''Ye were redeemed, not with corruptible things, with silver or gold, from your vain manner of life handed down from your fathers; but with precious blood, as of a lamb without blemish and without spot, even the blood of Christ'' (I Pet. 1:18, 19).

9. Paul also states that *we have redemption through the blood of Christ:* ''In whom we have our redemption through his blood, the forgiveness of our trespasses, according to the riches of his grace'' (Eph. 1:7).

10. *John's vision of the redeemed host* consisted of those who had ''washed their robes, and made them white in the blood of the lamb'' (Rev. 7:14).

III. HOW WE ARE CLEANSED BY THE BLOOD

All men who respect the Bible readily admit that sinful man is saved by the blood of Christ. There is no controversy here. But the fact that Christ shed his blood for all men (Heb. 2:9) and that only the minority will be saved (Matt. 7:13,14) is certain proof that there is something for man to do in order to obtain the forgiveness and blessings afforded by the shed blood of the Saviour. The question is: Upon what conditions does the blood cleanse from sin?

1. *In Jno. 19:34 we learn that Jesus shed his blood in his death.* This being true, man must come into Christ's death to reach the redeeming blood. Is this possible? Yes! Paul has made plain the way of entrance into Christ's death, the place where the blood was shed. Hear him: "Or are ye ignorant that all we who were baptized into Christ Jesus were baptized into his death? We were buried therefore with him through baptism into death: that like as Christ was raised from the dead through the glory of the Father, so we also might walk in newness of life" (Rom. 6:3,4). It is in baptism, in this age, that man comes in contact with the saving blood. Thus we marvel not that Jesus stipulated baptism as a condition of salvation (Mk. 16:16); that Peter said baptism was for the remission of sins (Acts 2:38); that Ananias commanded Paul to be baptized and wash away his sins (Acts 22:16). We are not surprised at such statements when we recall that the penitent believer is baptized into Christ's death, the place where the blood was shed, and thereby contacts the cleansing power.

2. *In Acts 20:28 we are told of the realm in which the blood cleanses:* "Take heed unto yourselves, and to all the flock, in which the Holy Spirit hath made you bishops, to feed the church of the Lord which he purchased with his own blood." The Lord's blood was shed to purchase the

Lord's church. It is, therefore, an accepted fact that if a man is redeemed and purchased by the blood of Christ, it must be by virtue of his connection and relationship to the church purchased by the blood. The fact that all of Christ's blood went into the purchase of Christ's church is proof that I must be in that church to be a beneficiary of the blood. God added to the blood-bought church only those who had believed, repented and had been baptized unto the remission of sins (Acts 2:37-47). Thus it stands that man today must believe, repent and be baptized for the remission of sins to receive the cleansing efficacy of the blood. When this is done God adds him to the church. It is here that he enjoys the promise of salvation; for Paul declares, "For the husband is the head of the wife, as Christ also is the head of the church, being himself the saviour of the body" (Eph. 5:23).

3. John has taught us *how the blood may keep us clean:* "But if we walk in the light, as he is in the light, we have fellowship one with another, and the blood of Jesus his Son cleanseth us from all sin" (I Jno. 1:7). John was speaking of Christians, members of the blood-bought church. If the members "walk in the light," do the will of God, they are brought into "fellowship one with another, and the blood of Jesus his Son cleanseth us from all sin"; i. e., continues to cleanse us and keeps us clean. What a glorious promise! But walking "in the light as he is in the light" is the condition on which the promise is suspended. Whoever has turned from the light of Christ's teaching has, therefore, "counted the blood of the covenant wherewith he was sanctified an unholy thing, and hath done despite unto the Spirit of grace" (Heb. 10:29).

115

REASON XVII

BECAUSE IT TEACHES THAT A CHANGE OF HEART IS INDISPENSABLE TO MAN'S SALVATION

I. INTRODUCTION

A RELIGION which does not touch and change the heart is not the religion given by the Christ. The heart is the spring from which our actions flow. If the heart has been defiled by sin, a black and wicked conduct flows therefrom. "For out of the heart come forth evil thoughts, murders, adulteries, fornications, thefts, false witness, railings" (Matt. 15:19). These heinous sins are first committed in the heart. If the fountain is kept pure, the stream will be pure. If man's heart is kept pure, his life will be pure. This should be sufficient to prove the absolute necessity of a change of heart. However, the charge has been made that the members of the church of Christ do not believe in a change of heart. The reader immediately recognizes the accusation to be false and unjust. The charge has doubtless grown out of man's ignorance of what the heart is, the analysis and exercises of it, and how it is changed, rather than out of maliciousness. This subject is one of the most discussed and least understood of all sermon topics. But God cannot be blamed for this confusion, for the Scriptures present the subject in a plain and comprehensible manner.

II. THE TWOFOLD NATURE OF MAN

The term *heart* is defined as the seat of life. The outward and visible man's heart is the hollow muscular organ in the left side, which keeps up the circulation of blood. Many have spoken of this lobe of flesh as though it were the subject of the gospel. How many times we have seen men pound themselves on the left chest and hear them exclaim, ''I feel it right here!'' They speak of the change of heart as though it were the heart of flesh in the chest cavity. Their misunderstanding has arisen in their failure to observe that the Bible teaches that man is both an outward and inward being, physical and spiritual, and that each has a seat of life or heart. Paul, in speaking of the dual nature of man, says, ''But though our outward man is decaying, yet our inward man is renewed day by day'' (II Cor. 4:16). When the heart of the outward or physical man is pricked, death follows. We have an example of this in II Sam. 18:14: ''He took three darts in his hand, and thrust them through the heart of Absalom.'' But when the heart of the inward or spiritual man is pricked, the outward man is untouched. For instance: ''Now when they heard this, they were pricked in their heart, and said unto Peter and the rest of the apostles, Brethren, what shall we do'' (Acts 2:37)? The hearts of these Jews were pricked with the gospel and they lived. Absalom's heart was pricked with darts and he died. The two different hearts were acted upon by two different weapons. It was the heart of the inward man that the gospel touched. It is evident that this is the heart which is changed in conversion to God. This fact is made still plainer by studying the analysis of the heart and its exercises.

WHY I AM A MEMBER OF THE CHURCH OF CHRIST

III. THE ANALYSIS AND EXERCISES OF THE HEART

1. *The heart is that part of man called intellect, which:*

(1) Thinks. "Wherefore think ye evil in your hearts" (Matt. 9:4)?

(2) Reasons. "Why reason ye these things in your hearts" (Mk. 2:8)?

(3) Understands. "Understand with their heart" (Matt. 13:15).

(4) Believes. "With the heart man believeth" (Rom. 10:10).

The Bible says that the human heart thinks, reasons, understands and believes. God calls this part of man the heart, but man calls it the intellect. So what the Bible ascribes to the heart, man attributes to the intellect.

2. *The heart is also seen to be that attribute of man called emotion, which:*

(1) Despises. "She despised him in her heart" (II Sam. 6:16).

(2) Desires. "Brethren, my heart's desire and my supplication to God is for them, that they may be saved" (Rom. 10:1).

(3) Loves. "Thou shalt love the Lord thy God with all thy heart" (Matt. 22:37).

(4) Trusts. "Trust in Jehovah with all thine heart" (Prov. 3:5).

So what God calls the heart, man calls the emotions. We see that man's heart embraces man's feelings, sensibilities or emotions. God's word says the heart despises, desires, loves and trusts.

3. *The heart is that quality of man called will, which:*

118

(1) Determines. "Hath determined this in his own heart" (I Cor. 7:37).

(2) Intends. "The thoughts and intents of the heart" (Heb. 4:12).

(3) Purposes. "That with purpose of heart they would cleave unto the Lord" (Acts 11:23).

(4) Obeys. "Ye became obedient from the heart" (Rom. 6:17).

So the heart determines, intends, purposes and obeys. Man calls this quality the will or volition. God calls it the heart.

4. *The heart is that faculty of man called conscience, which:*

(1) Condemns or condemns not. "If our heart condemn us, God is greater than our heart, and knoweth all things. Beloved, if our heart condemn us not, we have boldness toward God" (I Jno. 3:20,21).

The Bible speaks of a part of man which condemns or approves. God calls this part the heart. Man speaks of it as the conscience.

The above scriptures make it plain that the heart of the inward man is that part of man which embraces the intellect, emotions, will and conscience. It includes the whole of man's inner nature.

IV. CHANGE OF HEART

1. *A complete change is needed.* If the human heart embraces the intellect, emotions, will and conscience, there can be no complete change of heart until each has been changed. Each must be changed, if man's whole heart is changed. The heart must be changed from evil thoughts to

good thoughts, from wicked reasoning to good reasoning, from ignorance of God's word to a knowledge of it, from unbelief to belief, from despicableness to admiration, from the detestation of good to its desire, from the love of the world to the love of the Lord, from trust in material things to trust in God, from unrighteous determinations to righteous determinations, from unscriptural intentions to scriptural intentions, from unholy purposes to holy purposes, from disobedience to obedience, and from a condemning conscience to an approving conscience. This is the change of heart which is essential to man's salvation.

2. *How is the human heart changed?*

(1) The intellect is changed by evidence or testimony. It is changed from one state to another according to the evidence presented. Thomas' thoughts, reasoning, understanding and faith were not changed until Jesus appeared and said to him, "Reach hither thy finger, and see my hands; and reach hither thy hand, and put it into my side: and be not faithless but believing." Thomas then exclaimed, "My Lord and my God" (Jno. 20:24-29). Consider another example: Not so long ago the father and mother of a sailor received a telegram from Washington stating that their son was killed in the Pearl Harbor attack. Their thoughts, reasoning, understanding and faith were wholly changed. A few weeks later they received another telegram from the same authority saying that the first was all a mistake and that the boy was alive. This testimony produced another change in intellect. Thus it is easy to see that evidence or testimony controls the intellect. The word of God is the testimony God has given to change man's intellect: "These are written that ye may believe"

120

(Jno. 20:31). Again, "So belief cometh of hearing, and hearing by the word of Christ" (Rom. 10:17).

(2) The emotions are changed by faith in the testimony presented. It is the testimony believed that produces the change in emotions. Despicableness, desire, love and trust are the effects of the thing believed. The mother and father spoken of in the above paragraph had gladness turned to sadness and vice versa because of the thing believed. It is faith in the testimony of Christ that produces the change in the sinner's emotions from the desire of evil to the desire of good, from the love of the world to the love of Christ, and from trust in material things to trust in the Lord.

(3) The will is changed by motives produced by faith. Saul determined, intended and purposed not to obey Christ, thinking that He was an imposter. We see this persecutor with a determined will traveling on the road to Damascus to persecute Christians. Saul had no New Testament to read, but the audible word of Christ changed his heart from unbelief to belief. When he was told to be baptized and wash away his sins (Acts 22:16), he unhesitatingly obeyed. A disobedient heart was changed by motives produced by faith: belief in the goodness of Christ (Rom. 2:4), a motive; belief in the reward of the obedient (Heb. 5:9), a motive; belief in the punishment of the disobedient (Rev. 20:15), a motive. Saul's sins were washed away in the act of obedience. An obedient heart is indispensable to man's salvation. One becomes free from sin and a servant of righteousness by obeying from the heart: "Whereas ye were servants of sin, ye became obedient from the heart to that form of teaching whereunto ye

were delivered; and being made free from sin, ye became the servants of righteousness" (Rom. 6:17,18). The degree of faith which leads to salvation is a belief with all the heart which incites complete obedience from the heart. No man is a servant of Christ until he obeys from the heart. No heart is right until it is an obedient heart.

(4) The conscience is changed by faith in having done right. If a man understands and believes what Christ has commanded, he can never have an approving conscience until he does it. For instance, baptism is a command (Acts 10:48); this being true, if one understands and believes baptism is a command to be obeyed in order to enjoy the remission of sins (Acts 2:38), he cannot have a clear conscience until he has been baptized: "Which also after a true likeness doth now save you, even baptism, not the putting away of the filth of the flesh, but the interrogation of a good conscience toward God, through the resurrection of Jesus Christ (I Pet. 3:21). It is faith in having done right, having obeyed the commands of God, that changes the condemning conscience. The conscience does not hurt until one believes he has done wrong. This is why multitudes are in disobedience to God with an approving conscience. They just do not know or believe they are living in disobedience. This was true of Saul. He, with a conscience as clear as crystal (Acts 23:1), persecuted Christians, and did not have a condemning conscience until he learned and believed the truth. Saul's condemning conscience was then changed to a state of approval by obeying Christ.

When man's intellect, emotions, will and conscience are changed, man's whole heart is changed. It is evident that some who have talked the most about ''heartfelt religion,'' a changed heart, have really said the least. They preach only a partial change of heart, telling the people that belief only, a changed intellect, is the only essential item in man's salvation. But conversion to God demands a change of the whole heart. Such includes a change of intellect, emotions, will and conscience. Is it not, then, easy to see which religious organization preaches the religion of the whole heart?

REASON XVIII

BECAUSE OF ITS TEACHING AND PRACTICE CONCERNING PRAYER

I. INTRODUCTION

THE modernists among us do not emphasize prayer. This is due to their little faith. Prayer is a severe test of faith in God and his word. To the man void of faith, prayer is a vain cry in the wilderness with no one to answer; but to a man of faith, it is an address to God who has the ability to respond. Many religionists, however, who emphasize prayer—teach it, talk about it, pray at home, pray in the public worship and pray around the mourner's bench—have not learned that God has established certain conditions for a man to meet before his prayers are answered.

II. THE CHURCH OF THE FIRST CENTURY WAS A PRAYING CHURCH

1. In speaking of *three thousand who had been added to the church,* Luke says, "And they continued steadfastly ... in prayers" (Acts 2:41,42).

2. *The company of Christians, joined by Peter and John* who had been threatened by the Jewish council, "lifted up their voice to God with one accord" (Acts 4:24).

3. At the time *the twelve* gave instructions concerning the selection of men to serve tables, they said, "But we will continue steadfastly in prayer, and in the ministry of the word" (Acts 6:4).

4. When Peter was kept in prison by Herod *"prayer was made earnestly of the church unto God for him"* (Acts 12:5).

5. *Paul and Silas,* while prisoners in jail at Philippi during a midnight scene, prayed and sang hymns unto God (Acts 16:25).

6. When *Paul* had concluded his speech unto *the Ephesian elders,* "he kneeled down and prayed with them all" (Acts 20:36).

7. *The whole church at Tyre* kneeled down on the beach and prayed and bade Paul and his companions farewell (Acts 21:4,5).

8. *The churches were admonished to pray:* (1) To the saints in Rome: "Continuing steadfastly in prayer" (Rom. 12:12). (2) To the church of God in Corinth: "Give yourselves unto prayer" (I Cor. 7:5). (3) To the saints and faithful in Christ Jesus at Ephesus: "With all prayer and supplication praying at all seasons in the Spirit, and watching thereunto in all perseverance and supplication for all the saints" (Eph. 6:18). (4) To the church at Philippi: "In everything by prayer and supplication with thanksgiving let your requests be made known unto God" (Phil. 4:6). (5) To the saints and faithful brethren in Christ at Colossae: "Continue steadfastly in prayer, watching therein with thanksgiving" (Col. 4:2). (6) To the church of the Thessalonians: "Pray without ceasing; in everything give thanks: for this is the will of God in Christ Jesus to youward (I Thess. 5:17,18).

The foregoing is evidence that the church of Christ from the very beginning has been a praying institution. Hence, no group of people can be identified as the apostolic church unless prayer has the scriptural and proper place in the function of that body.

9. *Jesus*, the founder of the church, *believed in prayer and prayed much:* (1) At the beginning of his public ministry, immediately following his being baptized, he prayed (Lk. 3:21). (2) On the night before Jesus selected the twelve "he went out into the mountains to pray; and he continued all night in prayer to God" (Lk. 6:12). (3) "And after he had sent the multitudes away, he went up into the mountain apart to pray; and when even was come, he was there alone" (Matt. 14:23). (4) "And in the morning, a great while before day, he rose up and went out, and departed into a desert place, and there prayed" (Mk. 1: 35). (5) "But he withdrew himself in the desert, and prayed" (Lk. 5:16). (6) At the conclusion of Christ's parting message to the disciples he lifted up his eyes to heaven and prayed (Jno. 17). (7) Shortly before the trying ordeal of his arrest by the cruel mob he took Peter, James and John and went into the Garden of Gethsemane and prayed three times. (Matt. 26:36-44). (8) While he was dying upon the cross he prayed (Lk. 23:34-46).

Since Jesus, the founder of the church, spent much time in prayer, it follows that if we would be true members of his church we must also constantly engage in prayer. Surely no prayerless person can be a follower of Him who prayed so much.

III. GOD'S ANSWER TO PRAYER IS CONDITIONAL

Many religious bodies which have emphasized the importance of prayer have never preached the specified, scriptural conditions men must meet before their prayers will be heard. Let us not forget that men can pray and not be heard. James said, ''Ye ask and receive not, because ye ask amiss, that ye may spend it in your pleasures'' (Jas. 4:3). Not all who pray are heard, but all would be heard if there were no conditions attached. Note the following conditions of acceptable prayer·

1. *Be righteous.* ''For the eyes of the Lord are upon the righteous, and his ears unto their supplication'' (I Pet. 3:12).

2. *Keep God's commandments.* ''And whatsoever we ask we receive of him, because we keep his commandments and do the things that are pleasing in his sight'' (I Jno. 3:22). The negative of this is that the prayers of those who do not keep the commandments will not be answered.

3. *Pray in faith.* ''But let him ask in faith, nothing doubting: for he that doubteth is like the surge of the sea driven by the wind and tossed. For let not that man think that he shall receive anything of the Lord'' (Jas. 1:6,7). We must believe in God and believe that he will give what he has promised to give. If we ask for things God has not promised to give, we ask without faith; for faith cometh by hearing God's word (Rom. 10:17).

4. *Pray in Jesus' name.* ''And whatsoever ye shall ask in my name, that will I do, that the Father may be glorified in the Son. If ye shall ask anything in my name, that will I do'' (Jno. 14:13,14).

5. *Pray in harmony with God's will.* ''And this is the boldness which we have toward him, that, if we ask anything according to his will, he heareth us'' (I Jno. 5:14).

But if we ask according to our will instead of the divine will, we shall not receive.

6. *Have a forgiving spirit.* "But if ye forgive not men their trespasses, neither will your father forgive your trespasses" (Matt. 6:15). God will never answer our prayers unless we forgive those who trespass against us.

7. *Must be in the proper spiritual condition.* "If ye abide in me, and my words abide in you, ask whatsoever ye will, and it shall be done unto you" (Jno. 15:7). Our hearts must be the receptacles of Christ's word for our prayers to be answered.

8. *Pray with the right motive in mind.* "Ye ask, and receive not, because ye ask amiss, that ye may spend it in your pleasures" (Jas. 4:3). Prayers that are the outgrowth of wrong motives will not be heard.

IV. PRAYING FOR SINNERS

1. *Praying for sinners is a prevalent practice and needs much study.* We have seen that man must meet certain spiritual conditions to pray acceptably. Should such persons pray for sinners? (1) Jesus prayed for the sinful mob which crucified him: "Father, forgive them; for they know not what they do" (Lk. 23:34). (2) Jesus taught us to pray for sinners, saying, "But I say unto you, Love your enemies, and pray for them that persecute you" (Matt. 5:44). (3) Paul prayed for Israel: "Brethren, my heart's desire and my supplication to God is for them, that they may be saved" (Rom. 10:1).

We have seen that it is scriptural to pray for sinners. In so doing, we are following the teaching of Jesus and the examples of both Jesus and Paul. This brings us to the next question and division of study.

2. *Shall we sanction the mourner's bench system of religion?*

(1) An explanation is perhaps in order: The mourn-er's bench system is that of praying for alien sinners to be saved without obeying the conditions of salvation. This is a popular practice throughout the land. Penitent sin-ners are called to the mourner's bench where long and sincere prayers are prayed that they may be saved in their present condition without complying with the law of par-don. Will God do it? Will God set aside his law and will to obey their will?

(2) In answering the question we note the following rule of action which is true in both the physical and spiri-tual realms: When God ordains a law with which a man may comply and receive a blessing, it is an abomination to ask for the blessing without obeying the law. Solomon said, "He that turneth away his ear from hearing the law, even his prayer is an abomination" (Prov. 28:9).

By complying with the laws of nature a farmer may reap a harvest. Nature's law for reaping a harvest is this: Break the soil, prepare it for planting, plant the seed and cultivate the crop. Suppose the farmer wants God to give him a harvest without obeying this law, and he asks God for the harvest independent of the established conditions. Will God give it to him? No! Not only would such a prayer not be answered, but it would actually be an abom-ination. If he wants the harvest, let him obey the law. Of course one should pray, too,—"Give us this day our

129

daily bread"—because he could comply with the conditions for obtaining a harvest and not receive it.

(3) Does God have a law of pardon? If God has a law of pardon with which a man may comply and be saved, it is worse than useless to ask God to save a man before he complies with that law. It would be an abomination (Prov. 28:9). Such a prayer would be the equivalent of asking God to set aside his law and to ignore his will to obey man's will. God has a law of pardon to aliens; it demands that they believe (Heb. 11:6), repent of their sins (Lk. 13:3), confess faith in Christ as the Son of God (Matt. 10:32; Acts 8:37), and be baptized unto the remission of sins or that sins may be washed away (Acts 2:38; 22:16). The mourner's bench system of religion does not tell the sinner the conditions of salvation and urge him to do it; it urges the poor penitent to come to the mourner's bench in rejection of God's law of pardon and pray that God will save him in his disobedience to God's law. Such a prayer is the equivalent of saying, "O God, not thy will be done, but my will be done." How unscriptural and preposterous! We are not surprised to find that there is no example in the Scriptures of any alien sinner ever having his sins prayed away. Alien sinners, wanting to know what to do to be saved, were not invited to the mourner's bench. (See Chapter XIV to learn what they were told.)

3. *What about Jesus' prayer for sinners?*

(1) While Jesus was dying on the cross he eloquently prayed, "Father, forgive them; for they know not what they do" (Lk. 23:34). Jesus always did the Father's will; thus we are sure that he did not ask God to save these

sinners in disobedience to the divine law. Observe, therefore, that Jesus did not say, "Father, forgive them now, right now, this very moment." We know that Jesus did not pray for them to be saved then, because the prayer was not answered then.

(2) When was the prayer answered? On the day of Pentecost, fifty days after it was prayed, it still was unanswered. Here is the proof: When God forgives sin, he remembers it against man no more forever (Heb. 10:17). God does not forgive a sin and then later bring it up against the man. On the day of Pentecost Peter charges these people with the murder of Christ, saying, "Let all the house of Israel therefore know assuredly, that God hath made him both Lord and Christ, this Jesus whom ye crucified" (Acts 2:36). The fact that this indictment is brought against them is proof that they had not been forgiven: if they had, God would have remembered it against them no more forever. On this day, however, they believed as a result of hearing the gospel and wanted to know what to do. Peter told them to repent and be baptized unto the remission of sins (Acts 2:38). Three thousand did this and the Lord added them to the church (Acts 2:41,47). They were then saved in obedience to the law of pardon, and the prayer of Jesus was answered.

In view of the above facts, it is evident that God will not answer our prayers in the behalf of sinners until they obey the law of pardon. How effectual and gracious is the scriptural prayer! But how useless and vain is every prayer that clashes with the will of God!

131

REASON XIX
BECAUSE IT TEACHES AND ADMINISTERS SCRIPTURAL BAPTISM

I. INTRODUCTION

THE fact that no person can be a member of any church excepting the Quakers and the Christian Scientists without submitting to something that is called baptism is proof that men consider the subject important. For this reason and for the scriptural reasons, we should give the subject sincere consideration. The writer has. It is one of my many reasons for being a member of the church of Christ; for I claim to be a member of the scriptural church, the church which is teaching the Scriptures, the whole counsel of God, in every item of doctrine and worship.

II. WHOM MAY WE BAPTIZE

The answer is scriptural subjects, the ones spoken of in the Scriptures. We shall list them:

1. *Taught persons:* "Go ye therefore, and make disciples of all the nations [teach all nations, King James Version], baptizing them into the name of the Father and of the Son and of the Holy Spirit" (Matt. 28:19).

2. *Believing persons:* "He that believeth and is baptized shall be saved; but he that disbelieveth shall be condemned" (Mk. 16:16).

3. *Penitent persons:* "And Peter said unto them, Repent ye, and be baptized every one of you . . . ." (Acts 2:38).

4. *Persons who have confessed Jesus as the Son of God.* The eunuch, before being baptized, confessed: "I believe that Jesus Christ is the Son of God" (Acts 8:37, King James Version). (1) This confession is to be made before men (Matt. 10:32). (2) It is to be made with the mouth (Rom. 10:10); this excludes making the confession by signing a card, or by holding up your hand when every one else in the audience, excepting the preacher, has his head bowed.

The above passages are specific in putting teaching, belief, repentance and the confession that Christ is the Son of God before baptism. Those who baptize infants have completely reversed the divine order, and are saying, "Baptize them now and let them be taught, believe, repent and confess when they grow up." There is no way in the world for man to baptize infants without reversing the divine arrangement and corrupting the word of God; because teaching, faith, repentance and confession are prerequisites of scriptural baptism.

It gives me joy to emphasize these scriptures in view of the fact that my brethren have been accused of believing in water salvation. We believe the Bible and it does not teach such. It teaches that teaching, faith, repentance and confession must precede baptism for it to be scriptural and effectual; if not scriptural, it is no baptism at all in God's sight. Being accused of believing in water salvation is strange in view of the fact that many who make the charge practice such themselves. For instance, if sprinkling water upon a baby blesses it, what blessed it? It was neither teaching, faith, repentance nor confession; so if it received a blessing from such, it was the water and the water only which blessed it. Now that is water blessing or salvation; many believe in it, but we do not. It is true that it is a means of getting more members, but it is also true that they come by generation instead of regeneration.

III. WHAT DOES BAPTISM REQUIRE

Sprinkling, pouring or immersing? Obviously not all three. The word "baptize" is a verb, and a verb expresses one specific action instead of several unsynonymous actions. Hence, the Bible never speaks of a mode of baptism. The only way we can account for this is that the word "baptize" is one specific act and tells exactly what is to be done. Sprinkling, pouring and immersing, each, is one distinct and specific act. If the word "baptize" means sprinkling, then it does not mean pouring and immersing; if it means pouring, then it does not mean sprinkling and immersing; if it means immersing then it does not mean sprinkling and pouring. If the word "baptize" does not mean one specific act—but means sprinkling, pouring and immersing, all three—then no person could be baptized until he has done all three. No person believes it means that. Only one action can possibly be right—is it sprinkling, pouring or immersing? In studying the Scriptures pertaining to the subject, as given in the chart, you can easily decide for yourself.

REQUIREMENTS OF EACH

BAPTISM	IMMERSION	SPRINKLING	POURING
Water (Acts 8:36)	Yes	Yes	Yes
Much water (Jno. 3:23)	Yes	No	No
A going unto the water (Acts 8:36)	Yes	No	No
A going down into the water (Acts 8:38)	Yes	No	No
That both the baptizer and the one to be baptized go down into the water (Acts 8:38, 39)	Yes	No	No
A burial (Rom. 6:4)	Yes	No	No
A resurrection (Col. 2:12)	Yes	No	No
A birth (Jno. 3:5)	Yes	No	No
Body washed (Heb. 10:22)	Yes	No	No
A coming up out of the water (Acts 8:39; Matt. 3:16)	Yes	No	No

Every man who sprinkles or pours for baptism must at the last day face the Scriptures referred to in the above chart. We shall be judged by them and by all others (Rev. 20:12).

There is no comfort in being able to find the word "sprinkle" in the Bible, because it is never used in connection with baptism: (1) "And I will sprinkle clean water upon you, and ye shall be clean; from all your filthiness, and from all your idols, will I cleanse you" (Ezek. 36:25). This was practiced under the law of Moses, and in Num. 19:1-10 we have a record of the preparation of the waters of cleansing or purification. It consisted of the ashes of a red heifer, her skin, flesh, blood, her dung, and cedar-wood, and hyssop and scarlet. (2) "So shall he sprinkle many nations" (Isa. 52:15). The word "startle" is given in the margin of the Revised Version instead of "sprinkle" and this is in perfect accord with the context.

IV. THE TESTIMONY OF OTHERS

1. *Martin Luther:* "Baptism is a Greek word, and may be translated immersion, as when we immerse something in water, that it may be wholly covered."

2. *John Calvin:* "The word baptize signifies to immerse, and it is certain that immersion was the practice of the ancient church."

3. *John Wesley:* "We are buried with him—alluding to the ancient manner of baptizing by immersion" (Wesley's Notes on Rom. 6:4).

4. *Lyman Coleman:* "The primary signification of the original is to dip, plunge, immerse; the obvious import of the noun is immersion."

5. *Edinburgh Encyclopedia:* "In the time of the

apostles the form of baptism was very simple. The person to be baptized was dipped in a river or vessel."

6. *Liddell and Scott:* "Baptizo: to dip in or under water."

7. *Thayer:* "Baptizo: to dip repeatedly, to immerse, submerge."

8. *The Greek Catholic Church* testifies that immersion was the original practice, and continues to practice immersion.

9. *The Roman Catholic Church* admits that immersion was the original practice.

10. *The Church of England* admits that immersion was the original practice.

11. *The Methodist Church* approves of immersion and immerses those who request it.

12. *Webster's Dictionary:* "To dip or immerse in water, or to pour or sprinkle water upon." There is nothing surprising about this, because it is the function of a dictionary to give the present-day usage of words. The word carries all three meanings today because of its usage; and if men should begin to put their feet in water and call that baptism, the dictionary would give that as one of the meanings, too.

V. ORIGIN OF UPSCRIPTURAL BAPTISM

1. *The first recorded case of baptism by affusion* is that of Novation, 251 A. D., who received such as he lay in bed. It was at first the exception to the rule, being administered to the sick only, but finally the exception became the accepted practice.

2. *Hear the testimony of Karl Hefele,* a learned Ro-

man Catholic bishop: "The church has always been tender toward the sick; and for that reason she introduced 'clinical' baptism."—*History of Church Councils*, page 153. It was called "clinical" baptism because it was administered to the sick. The Catholic Church claims no scriptural authority for sprinkling, but rather admits that she introduced it.

3. Sprinkling for baptism, however, *was not legalized by the Catholic Church until 1311 A. D.* We now quote: "The Council of Ravenna, 1311, legalized the baptism of sprinkling, but the practice of 'clinical' or bedside baptism had long been in use and had spread from the sick room to the churches."—*Johnson's Universal Cyclopedia*, Vol. 1, page 488.

The foregoing facts are not denied by any informed person, Catholic or Protestant. Those who practice sprinkling for baptism have no higher authority for it than the Roman Catholic Church. The Catholics claim that their church has the authority to alter the will of God and substitute sprinkling for baptism. I do not believe it! I contend that neither the Catholic Church nor any other church has the authority to change the will of God on any subject.

VI. WHY BE BAPTIZED

This question is often asked. It is worthy of careful examination and respectful consideration. The fact that baptism is spoken of and alluded to more than one hundred times in the New Testament is proof of its prominence in the Christian religion. No subject could be discussed so often and be a matter of indifference.

Man is not the proper tribunal to decide the question. We must carry the question to the Bible and there seek its answer, and all who wish to be guided by the Lord will be satisfied. Here are some of the reasons found in God's word:

1. Christ had no sins and with him it was to fulfill all righteousness (Matt. 3:15).
2. It is commanded (Acts 10:48; Matt. 28:19).
3. It is the answer of a good conscience (I Pet. 3:20,21).
4. That one may rejoice (Acts 8:39; 16:33,34).
5. To get into Christ (Gal. 3:27).
6. To get into Christ's death (Rom. 6:3).
7. To be raised with Christ (Col. 2:12).
8. To walk in newness of life (Rom. 6:4).
9. To enter into the kingdom of God (Jno. 3:5).
10. To wash away sins (Acts 22:16).
11. To be saved (Mk. 16:16; I Pet. 3:21).
12. That one reject not the counsel of God (Lk. 7:30).
13. For or unto the remission of sins (Acts 2:38). It has been contended by some who have attempted to evade the essentiality of baptism that the Greek word "eis" in this passage which has been translated "for" or "unto" has been mistranslated, and that it should be translated "because of." This would make it teach repentance and baptism because of the remission of sins rather than for or unto the remission of sins. We shall give you the passage in twenty-four different translations that you may have the verdict of the versions. To save space we shall omit all words not necessary to show the meaning of the Greek word "eis."

(1) King James: "Repent and be baptized . . . for the remission of sins."

(2) American Standard: "Repent ye, and be baptized . . . unto the remission of your sins."

(3) Rotherham's Emphasized: "But Peter [said] unto them: Repent ye! and be immersed . . . into remission of your sins."

(4) Modern Speech: " 'Repent,' replied Peter, 'and be baptized . . . with a view to the remission of your sins.' "

(5) Modern English: "Change your mind and be baptized . . . for a release of your sins."

(6) Twentieth Century: " 'Repent,' answered Peter, 'and be baptized... for the forgiveness of your sins.' "

(7) Anderson: "Repent, and be immersed . . . in order to the remission of your sins."

(8) Living Oracles: "Reform, and be each of you immersed in the name of Jesus Christ in order to the remission of sins."

(9) R. A. Knox's Translation (Catholic, copyright, 1944, by Sheed & Ward, Inc.): "Repent, Peter said to them, and be baptized . . . to have your sins forgiven."

(10) Centenary Translation of the New Testament, by Helen Barrett Montgomery (Published by the American Baptist Publication Society: " 'Repent,' answered Peter, 'and be baptized... for the remission of your sins.' "

(11) The Riverside New Testament, by William G. Ballantine: "Peter said to them: 'Repent and be baptized ... for the forgiveness of your sins.' "

(12) William Tyndale's Translation, 1534: "Peter

sayde vnto them: repent and be baptized . . . for the remission of synnes.''

(13) New Testament Translation, by George Campbell, James Macknight, and Philip Doddridge, 1828 (Church of Scotland): ''And Peter said to them, Reform, and be each of you immersed . . . in order to the forgiveness of [your] sins.''

(14) English Revised Version, 1881: ''And Peter said unto them, Repent ye, and be baptized . . . unto the remission of your sins.''

(15) American Bible Union Translation (1869): ''Repent, and be each of you immersed . . . unto the remission of sins.''

(16) Modern Readers' Bible (Moulton): ''Repent ye and be baptized, everyone of you . . . unto the remission of your sins.''

(17) Emphatic Diaglotte: ''Reform and be immersed . . . for the forgiveness of sins.''

(18) Moffat Translation: '' 'Repent,' said Peter, 'Let each of you be baptized . . . for the remission of your sins.' ''

(19) Goodspeed's Translation: ''You must repent, and every one of you be baptized . . . in order to have your sins forgiven.''

(20) Weymouth's Modern Speech (Robertson's Revision): '' 'Repent,' replied Peter, 'and be baptized every one of you. . . for the remission of your sins.' ''

(21) Syriac Version: ''Repent and be baptized . . . for the remission of sins.''

(22) Warrell's Translation of the New Testament

(From the press of the American Baptist Publication Society): "And Peter said to them, 'Repent, and be immersed . . . . unto the remission of your sins.' "

(23) Douay Version (Catholic): "Do penance, and be baptized, every one of you . . . for the remission of your sins."

(24) Wycliffe's Translation of the New Testament (translated in 1308 and is the oldest complete English translation: "And Petre saide to heem, Do you penaunce, and each of you be baptized in the name of Jesus Christ, (into) remission of your synnes; and ye schulen take the gilfte of the Hooli Goost."

Hence, he who says that Acts 2:38 teaches that baptism is "because of" the remission of sins is at variance with the scholarship of the world.

Men say that baptism is only a Christian duty, but it is not a Christian duty. All Christian duties are repeated often. It is a Christian duty to sing, but we cannot be relieved of that duty by singing one song in a lifetime. It is also a Christian duty to pray, but one prayer in a lifetime will not free us of that responsibility. All Christian duties are to be done over and over again. For the preachers who preach that baptism is a Christian duty to be consistent, they will have to baptize all of their members at least every week or two. The fact that baptism is a command to be obeyed only once in a lifetime is proof that it is not a Christian duty, but rather proof that it is a command to be obeyed in becoming a Christian. When obeyed scripturally, that command is behind one forever.

REASON XX

BECAUSE IT TEACHES THAT A CHILD OF GOD CAN SO SIN AS TO BE ETERNALLY LOST

I. INTRODUCTION

THE doctrine that a child of God cannot so sin as to be eternally lost is not a new doctrine by any means. It is even spoken of in the Bible. It was preached in the long, long ago by the serpent in the Garden of Eden; he is the author of it and first preached it to Adam and Eve. God said that in the day they ate of the forbidden fruit they would die. In contradiction, the subtle serpent said, "Ye shall not surely die" (Gen. 3:4). In current language, he was saying, "You shall not be condemned because it is impossible for you to fall and be lost." But we have the word of God, the suffering of man, and marble monuments galore which testify otherwise. Satan encouraged the fall by preaching the impossibility of apostasy. What a warning! For this reason and many others, I could never entertain the thought of being a participant in a religious system which teaches this doctrine.

II. THE BIBLE TEACHES THAT A CHILD OF GOD CAN FALL AND BE LOST

1. *There are things for the Christian to do to keep from falling*: "Wherefore, brethren, give the more diligence to make your calling and election sure: for if ye do these things ye shall never stumble" (II Pet. 1:10) or fall. What things? The things mentioned in the five previous verses. It unmistakably implies, therefore, that if one does

not do these things he will fall. The child of God is commanded to give diligence to make his calling and election sure. Thus the Christian's election is evidently not sure or such a command would not be enjoined upon him.

2. *The Corinthian Christians were admonished to take heed lest they fall:* "Wherefore let him that thinketh he standeth take heed lest he fall." (I Cor. 10:12). If one cannot fall, why was this command given? If you knew it were absolutely impossible for some man on a building to fall, you would not rush up and exclaim, "Take heed, brother, lest ye fall!" Neither would the Holy Spirit issue such a warning if it be impossible for a Christian to fall.

3. *Paul knew it was possible for him to be rejected.* He said, "I buffet my body, and bring it into bondage; lest by any means, after that I have preached to others, I myself should be rejected" (I Cor. 9:27). Paul knew it was possible for him to be lost; and to prevent it, he buffeted his body.

4. *A child of God can quit believing* and when he does he will start falling: "Take heed, brethren, lest haply there shall be in any one of you an evil heart of unbelief, in falling away from the living God" (Heb. 3:12).

5. *The Galatians were taught that a Christian can fall from grace:* "Ye are severed from Christ, ye who would be justified by the law: ye are fallen away from grace" (Gal. 5:4). In attempting to be justified by the law of Moses they became guilty of a complete apostasy. Not only is it possible for Christians to fall, but in this instance it actually happened, even though men say it is impossible. Note: (1) Man is saved by grace (Eph. 2:8). (2) A Christian may fall away from grace (Gal. 5:4). (3) Therefore, a Christian may be lost.

144

6. A Christian can so sin as to be eternally lost, because *he can so sin as to be in a worse condition than he was before he became a Christian*: "For if, after they have escaped the defilements of the world through the knowledge of the Lord and Saviour Jesus Christ, they are again entangled therein and overcome, the last state is become worse with them than the first. For it were better for them not to have known the way of righteousness, than, after knowing it, to turn back from the holy commandment delivered unto them. It is happened unto them according to the true proverb, The dog turning to his vomit again, and the sow that had washed to wallowing in the mire" (II Pet. 2:20-22). (1) They had escaped the defilements of the world. (2) They were again entangled therein and overcome. (3) The last state is worse than the first. If this is not proof that a Christian can so sin as to be eternally lost, then why is the last state worse than the first? Could the last state be worse than the first, if the person goes to heaven?

7. *The parable of the sower* emphatically refutes the doctrine of the impossibility of apostasy (Matt. 13:3-8; 18-23; Lk. 8:4-15): The seed in the parable is the word of God (Lk. 8:11). The sower is the gospel teacher or preacher (I Cor. 3:6). The soil is the human heart (Lk. 8:15). The wayside hearer did not become a Christian. The stony ground represents those who accepted the word but withered because of tribulation or persecution and temptation (Matt. 13:20,21; Lk. 8:13). They became Christians but failed to produce fruit. Their appointed lot is recorded in Matt. 7:19: "Every tree that bringeth not forth good fruit is hewn down, and cast into the fire." The thorny ground represents those who became Chris-

tians but were choked by the cares of the world, the deceitfulness of riches, or the pleasures of this life and became unfruitful (Matt. 13:22; Lk. 8:14). They accepted the word and later fell. The parable is a forceful warning to Christians that they can fall and be lost.

8. *The parable of the vine and the branches* is more proof that a branch in the vine, a Christian, can be burned: "Every branch in me that beareth not fruit, he taketh it away: and every branch that beareth fruit, he cleanseth it, that it may bear more fruit .... If a man abide not in me, he is cast forth as a branch, and is withered; and they gather them, and cast them into the fire, and they are burned" (Jno. 15:2-6). "Every branch in me," declares the Christ. "In me!" Not stuck on; but actually in me, the Christ. The argument, "If one falls, he was never in Christ," is recognized as loose talk when viewed in the light of this teaching. So the little phrase "in me" destroys one of the preachers' favorite arguments, and settles the controversy as to whether or not the lost branch was in Christ. What happens to the branch that does not bear fruit? "He taketh it away." Then what? After it is withered it will be cast into the fire. And the "fire" is the "hell of fire" (Matt. 5:22).

9. We learn from the *parable of the talents* that a servant of the Lord can be lost (Matt. 25:14-30): (1) The persons under consideration are the Lord's own servants. (2) Two were faithful and were blessed; one was unprofitable, wicked and slothful, and the Lord commanded that he be cast out into the outer darkness where there is weeping and gnashing of teeth. (3) Therefore, one of the Lord's own servants can be eternally lost.

10. *Jesus said that he would gather certain ones out*

146

of his kingdom and cast them into the furnace of fire: "The Son of man shall send forth his angels, and they shall gather out of his kingdom all things that cause stumbling, and them that do iniquity, and shall cast them into the furnace of fire: there shall be weeping and gnashing of teeth" (Matt. 13:41,42). The citizens of Christ's kingdom, newborn creatures, children of God, who cause stumbling and do iniquity shall be cast into the furnace of fire.

11. *Christ said that he would—so it is not impossible —spew the Laodiceans out of his mouth*: "So because thou art lukewarm, and neither hot nor cold, I will spew thee out of my mouth" (Rev. 3:16). Spewed out of Christ! So we can get out of Christ.

12. *Paul said that men would apostatize or fall away from the faith* (I Tim. 4:1-3). It is an evident conclusion that they had the faith or they could not have departed from it. The fate of those who depart from the faith is seen in I Tim. 5:12: "Having condemnation, because they have rejected their first pledge," or "Having condemnation, because they have cast off their first faith" (King James Version).

13. *A Christian's harvest will be dependent upon his sowing*: "Be not deceived; God is not mocked; for whatsoever a man soweth, that shall he also reap. For he that soweth unto his own flesh shall of the flesh reap corruption; but he that soweth unto the Spirit shall of the Spirit reap eternal life" (Gal. 6:7-9). This message was addressed to Christians; therefore the universal law of sowing and reaping applies to the Christian as well as to the sinner. A Christian may sow to the flesh and his harvest will be corruption; he may sow to the Spirit and his harvest will be eternal life, if he faints not. This law is unalterable.

147

14. *Believers may sin and be in danger of death*: "My brethren, if any among you err from the truth, and one convert him; let him know, that he who converteth a sinner from the error of his way shall save a soul from death, and shall cover a multitude of sins" (Jas. 5:19,20). (1) These were believers (Jas. 2:1): only such are in danger of death, because the unbelievers are already dead (Eph. 2:1,5). (2) Hence, believers can err from the truth and be in danger of death.

15. *We can sin against the brethren and cause them to perish*: "For through thy knowledge he that is weak perisheth, the brother for whose sake Christ died" (I Cor. 8:11). This death is the second death (Rev. 20:14) rather than the first or physical death which comes to all. No man lives who can harmonize this passage with the "once-saved-always-saved" theory.

16. *Many of Christ's disciples separated themselves from him*: "Upon this many of his disciples went back, and walked no more with him" (Jno. 6:66). (1) It is admitted that man cannot be saved apart from Christ (Jno. 15:5). (2) Many of Christ's disciples forever separated themselves from him (Jno. 6:66). (3) Therefore, these disciples of Christ were eternally lost.

17. *A child of God can be lost because he can lie, and die in that state.* Can he die in that condition? Ananias and Sapphira did (Acts 5). The fate of those who die in that condition is seen in Rev. 21:8: " . . . . and all liars, their part shall be in the lake that burneth with fire and brimstone; which is the second death" (Rev. 21:8). Therefore, it is possible for a child of God to sin and be eternally lost.

18. *It is either possible for a child of God to be lost or*

148

it is impossible for a child of God to ever taste death, under certain conditions. No drunkard "shall inherit the kingdom of God" (I Cor. 6:10). Can a child of God get drunk? You say, "Yes." But men say that God will not let him die in that condition. If that were true, a Christian could get drunk and stay drunk and never would die but would live forever right here on earth. What an absurdity!

19. *If a child of God cannot be lost, the devil is a fool.* He has been laboring for about six thousand years to damn the souls of the children of God; and if he has never succeeded in damning the soul of just one child of God, he is a simpleton for continuing.

III. AN EXAMINATION OF SOME PROOF TEXTS

1. *"Verily, verily, I say unto you, He that heareth my word, and believeth him that sent me, hath eternal life, and cometh not into judgment, but hath passed out of death into life"* (Jno. 5:24). This citation is used to prove that the believer has eternal life now, and hence it is impossible for him to be lost. We know that one scripture does not contradict another, so what is the explanation?

Jesus' statement concerning his shed blood will help: "For this is my blood of the covenant, which is poured out for many unto remission of sins" (Matt. 26:28). Christ spoke as if his blood had actually been poured out, while it still flowed in his veins; it was to be poured out in the future. Apparently, in Jno. 5:24, Jesus carried himself forward to the judgment day, and spoke as if it were present. The believers enjoy the promise of eternal life and will receive it; or, carrying himself forward to the judgment, the believer hath eternal life.

The believer has eternal life in two senses: (1) In promise (I Jno. 2:25). (2) And he has Jesus who is the

149

"eternal life, which was with the Father, and was manifested unto us" (I Jno. 1:2). However, the Bible teaches in many places that the believer upon this earth does not now have eternal life in its actuality, for instance: (1) Both eternal life and everlasting condemnation are on the other side of the valley of death (Dan. 12:2). (2) We are now in hope of eternal life (Tit. 1:1,2), and we do not hope for what we have (Rom. 8:25). (3) The Lord will render eternal life (Rom. 2:6,7). (4) Eternal life is to come in the end (Rom. 6:22). (5) The righteous will receive eternal life at the time the wicked receive eternal punishment (Matt. 25:46). (6) Eternal life is to be received in the world to come (Mk. 10:30).

2. *"Who shall separate us from the love of Chrsit? shall tribulation, or anguish, or persecution, or famine, or nakedness, or peril, or sword? . . . . For I am persuaded that neither death, nor life, nor angels, nor principalities, nor things present, nor things to come, nor powers, nor height, nor depth, nor any other creature, shall be able to separate us from the love of God, which is in Christ Jesus our Lord."* (Rom. 8:35-39). If the passage has reference to our love for God instead of God's love for us, it still does not teach the impossibility of apostasy; but rather that such external things cannot separate us from the love of God, but this is far short of teaching that we cannot separate ourselves from the love of God. It is plain that we can separate ourselves from the love of God: (1) "Abide ye in my love" (Jno. 15:9). (2) "If ye keep my commandments ye shall abide in my love" (Jno. 15:10). (3) "Keep yourselves in the love of God" (Jude 21). If you wish to say that the passage has reference to God's love for man, it

still does not prove the impossibility of apostasy; because the fact that God loves man is no proof of man's salvation, for God loved the whole world (Jno. 3:16) and he loved us while we were yet sinners (Rom. 5:8).

3. *"Whosoever is begotten of God doeth no sin, because his seed abideth in him: and he cannot sin, because he is begotten of God"* (I Jno. 3:9). John says that the person cannot sin because the seed abideth in him. The seed is the word of God (Lk. 8:11), and the devil can steal the word out of a person's heart (Lk. 8:12). John is not teaching in this verse that it is impossible for a Christian to sin, because he teaches in other plain verses that he can: (1) "If we say that we have no sin, we deceive ourselves, and the truth is not in us" (I Jno. 1:8). (2) "If we confess our sins, he is faithful and righteous to forgive us our sins, and to cleanse us from all unrighteousness" (I Jno. 1:9). (3) "My little children, these things write I unto you that ye may not sin" (I Jno. 2:1). (4) "If any man sin, we have an advocate with the Father, Jesus Christ the righteous" (I Jno. 2:1). The person who places an interpretation on one passage that contradicts other plain passages has surely misinterpreted it. Thus another proof text fails to prove!

4. *Rom. 7:15-25 is used in an effort to prove that it is the body of the Christian which sins and not his spirit.* If so—and if what a man sows he shall reap (Gal. 6:6,7)—then his body will be cast into hell while his spirit will go to heaven. Now this is something new under the sun: a man's spirit in heaven and his body in hell! The truth of the matter is as follows: (1) The spirit of man lets sin reign in the body (Rom. 6:12). (2) It is the spirit instead of the body that knows (I Cor. 2:11). (3) Some sins are com-

mitted to gratify the flesh, but they are first committed in the heart and proceed from the heart (Mk. 7:21-23).

5. *"If any man's work shall be burned, he shall suffer loss: but he himself shall be saved; yet so as through fire"* (I Cor. 3:15). The teacher's works which may be burned are the persons he converted. This would be a loss, but he himself could still be saved. The Corinthians were Paul's work and he feared that some might be lost. This verse disproves rather than proves the impossibility of apostasy.

6. *"Who by the power of God guarded through faith unto a salvation ready to be revealed in the last time"* (I Pet. 1:5). We are guarded by the power of God unto a salvation, and it is "through faith." The exertion of the power is of God; to believe is our part, and we shall do well to remember that man can quit believing (Heb. 3:12) and thus fail to be guarded by the power of God.

7. *Matt. 7:21-23 is used to prove that Christ does not know and has never known the ones who fall.* But the passage does not prove that. It only proves that Christ had never known these false prophets, for we learn in verse one of the paragraph that they are the ones under consideration.

8. *"They went out from us but they were not of us; for if they had been of us, they would have continued with us; but they went out, that they might be made manifest that they all are not of us"* (I Jno. 2:19). In verse eighteen we learn that John is speaking of antichrists. These antichrists had gone out from the apostles, preaching a different doctrine. This was proof that they were not of the apostles; if so, they would have continued with them, preaching the doctrine they preached; for the Holy Spirit which the apostles possessed would not have the apostles

152

preach one doctrine and these men preach something else. John says that "all" were not of us. Such were the ones these false teachers had drawn to themselves. So, all had not been with the apostles, while some had, even though they were not of the apostles.

9. *"There hath no temptation taken you but such as man can bear; but God is faithful, who will not suffer you to be tempted above that ye are able; but will with the temptation make also the way of escape, that ye may be able to endure it"* (I Cor. 10:13). God is faithful to make an opportunity of escape for the Christian, and the Christian must seize the opportunity or he will fall; for the preceding verse says, "Wherefore let him that thinketh he standeth take heed lest he fall."

10. *"My sheep hear my voice, and I know them, and they follow me; and I give unto them eternal life; and they shall never perish, and no one shall snatch them out of my hand"* (Jno. 10:27,28). These wonderful promises are conditional and dependent upon the person's following Christ: "they follow me." Jesus teaches in the twelfth verse of the chapter that the sheep can be snatched and scattered: "And the wolf snatcheth them and scattereth them."

The foregoing ten proof texts are not all the "once-saved-always-saved" folk offer, but are some of the main ones.

REASON XXI

BECAUSE IT TEACHES THAT INFANTS ARE BORN PURE AND INNOCENT RATHER THAN DEPRAVED

I. INTRODUCTION

MANY people have knowingly and unknowingly—the majority unknowingly—*subscribed to church creeds which teach hereditary total depravity.* Webster says that hereditary means "transmitted, or transmissible, as a constitutional quality or condition from parent to offspring"; and that depravity means "the state of being evil, perverted, corrupted." It is a theory which claims that sinful corruption has been transmitted to the infant from the parent and that it is wholly inclined to evil; that it is inherently impure; that it is a child of the devil.

2. *One error leads to another.* The doctrine of hereditary total depravity led to the erroneous doctrine of infant baptism. A quotation from John Wesley, the founder of the Methodist Church, is in order: "But the grand question is, Who are the proper subjects of baptism—grown persons only, or infants also? In order to answer this fully, I shall, first, lay down the grounds of infant baptism, taken from scripture, reason, and primitive universal practice; and, secondly, answer the objections against it.

"As to the grounds of it: If infants are guilty of original sin, then they are proper subjects of baptism; seeing, in the ordinary way, they cannot be saved, unless this be washed away by baptism. It has been already

154

proved, that this original stain cleaves to every child of man; and that thereby they are children of wrath, and liable to eternal damnation . . . . Infants need to be washed from original sin; therefore they are proper subjects of baptism."—*Wesley's Works, Miscellaneous,* Vol. 2, p. 16.

Neander also states that infant baptism evolved from the doctrine of original sin.—*Church History,* Vol. 1, pages 426, 427.

3. *It would be unjust* to leave the impression that advocates of infant baptism are the only ones who have taught hereditary total depravity. This would be unfair to the Baptists. Therefore we insert a quotation from their church manual: "We believe that man was created in holiness, under the law of his Maker; but by voluntary transgression fell from that holy and happy state; in consequence of which all mankind are now sinners, not by constraint but choice; being by nature utterly void of that holiness required by the law of God, positively inclined to evil; and therefore under just condemnation to eternal ruin, without defence or excuse."—*Church Manual Designed For The Use of Baptist Churches,* by J. M. Pendleton, page 46. "All mankind" leaves out no body. It includes infants as well as adults.

4. *No blacker picture* can be painted than this which has been painted by the advocates of hereditary total depravity. The writer could never affiliate with a group which teaches this unscriptural and repugnant doctrine.

II. AN EXAMINATION OF SOME PROOF TEXTS

1. *The advocates of this theory often use Psa.* 14:2,3 as a proof text, but it disproves it instead: "Jehovah looked down from heaven upon the children of men, to see if there

were any that did understand, that did seek after God. They are all gone aside; they are together become filthy; there is none that doeth good, no, not one." This proves that the people were very wicked, but does not prove that they were born in this state. The passage says, "They are all gone aside; they are together become filthy." It would have been impossible for them to have gone aside and to have become filthy if they had been born that way. The fact that they went aside and became filthy is proof that they were not born that way.

2. *Psa.* 51:5, *another of their proof texts, does not teach it:* "Behold, I was brought forth in iniquity; and in sin did my mother conceive me." Those who advocate hereditary total depravity infer that David was born a sinner, but the passage is not even susceptible of that interpretation. Sin is mentioned in the verse, but it was committed before David existed. David did not exist when he was conceived. Hence, the iniquity and the sin spoken of existed before David had an existence.

3. *Paul's statement in Eph.* 2:3 is also relied on to prove this doctrine: ". . . . . and were by nature children of wrath, even as the rest" (Eph. 2:3). "By nature," however, does not always mean "by inheritance." Adam Clarke, a believer in hereditary depravity, would not use the verse as a proof text for it. He rather said, "The apostle appears to speak of sinful habits."

4. *We next examine Psa.* 58:3: "The wicked are estranged from the womb; they go astray as soon as they are born, speaking lies." This states that they went astray after they were born. They were not born astray. Their going astray consisted of speaking lies. Infants cannot speak lies; therefore this sin was not committed in infancy.

156

III. PASSAGES WHICH REFUTE THIS FALLACIOUS DOCTRINE

1. *Man became a sinner in youth rather than at birth*: "Jehovah said in his heart, I will not again curse the ground any more for man's sake, for that the imagination of man's heart is evil from his youth" (Gen. 8:21). If man's heart became evil in youth, then it must have been pure before youth.

2. *Man's spirit has been given to him by his Maker*: "And the dust returneth to the earth as it was, and the spirit returneth unto God who gave it" (Eccl. 12:7). If God has given man a corrupted spirit, then is it not unfair and unjust for God to hold man responsible for his corruption?

3. *An infant is not depraved because God is not depraved.* Paul said in that famous speech at Mars' Hill, "For we are also his offspring" (Acts 17:28). Being the offspring of God, a child is not depraved unless God is depraved. No one could accuse God of being depraved. Then why make the accusation against His offspring?

4. The Holy Spirit declares that *the child shall not bear the iniquity of the parent*: "The soul that sinneth it shall die: the son shall not bear the iniquity of the father, neither shall the father bear the iniquity of the son; the righteousness of the righteous shall be upon him, and the wickedness of the wicked shall be upon him" (Ezek. 18:20). Look what we have in this verse: First, both righteousness and iniquity rest upon its doer and not upon another. Justice demands this. Second, "the son shall not bear the iniquity of the father." Those who insist that the child must bear the iniquity of father (Adam) flatly contradict this statement.

157

5. A little child is not depraved, because *man must become as a little child to enter into the kingdom of heaven*: Jesus said, "Except ye turn and become as little children, ye shall in no wise enter into the kingdom of heaven" (Matt. 18:3). Yet many religionists teach that a child is hereditarily totally depraved. Was Jesus teaching that a man must become wicked and corrupted to enter into the kingdom of heaven? Of course not.

6. *David was not of the belief* that his child died with a corrupted nature and guilty of sin. Contrariwise, he said, "I shall go to him, but he will not return to me" (II Sam. 12:23).

7. *It is impossible for sin to be inherited*: Sin is a violation of God's law by either commission or omission. Concerning commission: "Whosoever committeth sin transgresseth also the law: for sin is the transgression of the law" (I Jno. 3:4, K. J.V.). Relative to omission: "To him therefore that knoweth to do good, and doeth it not, to him it is sin" (Jas. 4:17). Sin is either a transgression or omission of law. This being true, it is absolutely impossible for man to inherit it because it is not an inherent quality.

8. *The fact that God has not given a plan for saving infants* is certain proof that they are not lost, that they are not sinners.

REASON XXII

BECAUSE IT TEACHES THAT THE MIRACULOUS MANIFESTATIONS OF THE SPIRIT HAVE CEASED

I. INTRODUCTION

MANY religious bodies today affirm that they speak by inspiration and perform miracles. Such preaching has occasioned much confusion in the minds of many, and a study of the subject is now in order. If the Bible teaches that miraculous gifts were to continue through the centuries, then I am with the wrong group; but if it teaches that such gifts were to terminate at the accomplishment of a certain work, then all who claim this power are in error. It must be one or the other; and to the Scriptures, therefore, we must go.

II. CHRIST WORKED MANY MIRACLES

1. *Jesus had to perform miracles to establish the claim that he was the Son of God.* If there had been no miraculous signs accompanying his work, men would have had no assurance that he was the Messiah. The power to perform miracles stamped Christ's work with a divine seal. Nicodemus, a ruler of the Jews, readily admitted it by saying, "Rabbi, we know that thou art a teacher come from God; for no man can do these signs that thou doest, except God be with him" (Jno. 3:2). With such divine credentials, he was recognized as "a teacher come from God."

2. Jesus' claim demanded miracles and *he established the claim by even doing "many other signs . . . .* which

are not written in this book" (Jno. 20:30). However, many signs are written and some of them are: (1) the blind received their sight (Jno. 9:1-12); (2) the lame were made to walk (Matt. 21:14); (3) the lepers were cleansed (Lk. 17:11-19); (4) the deaf were made to hear (Mk. 7:31-37); (5) the sick were healed (Matt. 8:14-17); (6) demons were cast out (Matt. 8:28-34); (7) he walked on the water (Matt. 14:22-33); (8) the wind and sea obeyed him (Matt. 8:27); (9) thousands were fed with only a few loaves and fishes (Matt. 14:13-21); (10) he raised the dead (Jno. 11:32-45); and (11) he went beyond all this and made the evidence impregnable forever in that he died and arose from the dead (Jno. 20:19-31), showing himself alive after his passion by many proofs (Acts 1:3).

3. *The warranted signs of Christ were recorded for the purpose of producing faith*: "Many other signs therefore did Jesus in the presence of the disciples, which are not written in this book: but these are written, that ye may believe that Jesus is the Christ, the Son of God; and that ye may have life in his name" (Jno. 20:30,31). We see the purpose of recording some of the signs: to produce faith in Christ. Furthermore, we see why many other signs were not written: they were not needed for this purpose. All of this being true, then there is no need today for any manifestation of supernatural power to convince man of the divinity of Christ. Hence, to ask for a miraculous manifestation today that you may believe in Christ is nothing short of an insult to Him who has already given the means to produce faith.

160

III. THE INSPIRATION AND CONFIRMATION OF THE MESSAGE

1. *It was indispensable* that the first preachers of the gospel be inspired to know what to say, and that they perform miracles to confirm what was said. There was no other way, because there was no written New Testament confirmed by miracles at that time. How else could men have known they were accepting the pure gospel?

2. In keeping with the needs characteristic of the beginning of the gospel, *the apostles were promised the baptism in the Holy Spirit that they might infallibly carry out the work begun by Jesus* (Acts 1:4,5). Here are some thoughts relative to the promise:

(1) The Holy Spirit would speak through the apostles: It shall be given you what ye shall speak; "for it is not ye that speak, but the Holy Spirit" (Mk. 13:11).

(2) The Holy Spirit would teach and give them a memory of what Jesus had taught: The Comforter "shall teach you all things, and bring to your remembrance all that I have said unto you" (Jno. 14:26).

(3) The Holy Spirit was to bear witness of Christ: " . . . shall bear witness of me" (Jno. 15:26).

(4) The Holy Spirit was to guide them into all truth: "Howbeit when he, the Spirit of truth, is come, he shall guide you into all the truth" (Jno. 16:13).

(5) The Holy Spirit would clothe them with power: "Ye are witnesses of these things. And behold, I send forth the promise of my Father upon you: but tarry ye in the city until ye be clothed with power from on high" (Lk. 24:48,49). This power with which they were to be clothed would take care of the proclamation of the true message, as demonstrated in the above verses; this power

161

would also enable them to perform miracles to confirm the truth of the message preached. The signs that were to accompany the preaching were promised at the time the eleven were commanded to go into all the world and preach the gospel: "And these signs shall accompany them that believe: in my name shall they cast out demons; they shall speak with new tongues; they shall take up serpents, and if they drink any deadly thing, it shall in no wise hurt them; they shall lay hands on the sick, and they shall recover" (Mk. 16:17,18). For what purpose were the signs to accompany the word? Here is the answer: "And they went forth, and preached everywhere, the Lord working with them, and confirming the word by the signs that followed (Mk. 16:20). Listen to Paul's reiteration of that purpose: " . . . . which having at the first been spoken through the Lord, was confirmed unto us by them that heard; God also bearing witness with them, both by signs and wonders, and by manifold powers, and by gifts of the Holy Spirit, according to his own will" (Heb. 2:3,4).

In the above quotations I have proved two things: *First,* it was necessary that the Holy Spirit come upon the apostles that the gospel might be proclaimed with infallible and unerring certainty; the revelation of the message of salvation could not be trusted to the fallible memories of fallible men. *Second,* it was essential that signs accompany them to the end that the message be authenticated.

3. *In Acts* 2:1-4 *we read of the coming of the Holy Spirit* upon the apostles, the fulfillment of the promise.

(1) It was promised that the Holy Spirit would guide them in the preaching. In Acts 2:4 we read that the Spirit gave them utterance.

(2) The Lord also promised that signs would accom-

pany them. In Acts 2:43 we read: " .... and many wonders and signs were done through the apostles."

One of the signs was the speaking with "new tongues" (Mk. 16:17). On this day, the day of Pentecost, the apostles spoke with "other tongues" (Acts 2:4). There were Jews present from every nation under heaven (2:5), and "every man heard them speaking in his own language" (2:6). They marveled and said, "And how hear we, every man in our own language wherein we were born?" (2:8). They also said, "....we hear them speaking in our tongues the mighty works of God" (2:11). We see that this speaking in tongues was not a lot of unintelligible sounds, but was the speaking in languages that could be understood by the people who lived in the various countries where such languages were common. Those who claim to speak in "unknown tongues" today should speak in languages they have never been taught rather than put on an exhibition of nonsensical utterances. Let one who has never learned Spanish, French and Latin speak in these languages. Yes, let him.

A few years ago, in talking to a lady on this subject, I pulled a letter from my pocket and handed it to her, saying, "This letter might help you." She read the first part, which was in English, and then asked, "What is the other half of this letter?" I replied, "It is the unknown tongue." She marveled and said, "Can you read this? Can you interpret it?" I did. She continued, "We can speak it, but not a one of us can write it or read it." I then explained: "Lady, this is just plain old Spanish, but to you it is an unknown tongue, a tongue you have never learned. The people on the day of Pentecost heard in their own tongues or languages wherein they were born. They

163

did not hear a tongue that was never known by anybody at any time or place. They heard in tongues or languages that could be written as well as spoken.''

The speaking in tongues was only one of the signs that followed them. They healed the sick, cast out demons and did many other wonders.

4. *The coming of the Holy Spirit upon the Gentiles* (Acts 10:44-48)—Cornelius and his friends—*was for a different purpose.* It was the baptism in the Holy Spirit, for Peter identified it as such (Acts 11:15,16).

(1) The purpose of this baptism is clearly seen in the use that was later made of it. At Jerusalem, Peter related the incident to remove the doubts which the Jews had as to the propriety of baptizing Gentiles (Acts 11:1-18); therefore this is unquestionably the design of it: *a design external to themselves.* This being the purpose, when it was demonstrated once, there was no need for it to be repeated; herein is the reason it did not occur again.

(2) This baptism in the Spirit did not save Cornelius and his friends. They—the same as the Jews on Pentecost—had to hear the gospel and be saved by it. The angel had previously told Cornelius that Peter "shall speak unto thee words, whereby thou shalt be saved, thou and all thy house" (Acts 11:13,14). So they were saved by words rather than by the baptism of the Holy Spirit.

IV. ONLY THE APOSTLES HAD POWER TO CONFER THE MIRACULOUS GIFTS OF THE SPIRIT

The power to bestow the miraculous gifts of the Spirit on Christians was peculiar to the apostles. No one else enjoyed this honor, and those who received these gifts from the apostles could not transfer them to others. The proof is next in order:

1. *The Samaritans received the miraculous gifts of the Spirit through two apostles*: "Now when the apostles that were at Jerusalem heard that Samaria had received the word of God, they sent unto them Peter and John: who, when they were come down, prayed for them, that they might receive the Holy Spirit: for as yet it was fallen upon none of them: only they had been baptized into the name of the Lord Jesus. Then laid they their hands on them, and they received the Holy Spirit" (Acts 8:14-17). These Samaritans had been baptized—therefore they had received the gift of the Holy Spirit as promised in Acts 2:38—but they had not received miraculous power. The apostles sent Peter and John to lay hands on them that they might have the power. Why did not Philip—a man who had done many signs in their midst (Acts 8:5-8)—bestow this power on them? The answer is apparent: Since he was not an apostle, he could not. If so, why were two apostles sent to confer it?

2. *Philip received this miraculous power as a result of the laying on of apostolic hands.* It has been mentioned that many signs accompanied Philip's preaching at Samaria (Acts 8:5-8). Where did he get the power to perform miracles? Answer: He was one of the seven chosen to look after some benevolent work in the church at Jerusalem; "whom they set before the apostles: and when they had prayed, they laid their hands upon them" (Acts 6:1-6). It is plain that this power came to Philip through the laying on of the hands of the apostles.

3. *Paul conferred this power on twelve men he baptized.* In Acts 19:1-7 we read of twelve men baptized by Paul. They had, therefore, received the gift of the Holy Spirit (Acts 2:38), but they had not received the miraculous gifts of the Holy Spirit. This could come to them

165

only through the laying on of apostolic hands. Hence, " . . . . when Paul laid his hands upon them, the Holy Spirit came on them; and they spake with tongues, and prophesied" (Acts 19:6).

V. THE EXPIRATION OF MIRACULOUS POWER

1. We have seen in the above section that miraculous gifts could be conferred only by an apostle; no one else could. Therefore, when the last apostle died, the power to confer miraculous gifts expired and *when the last person on whom an apostle had laid hands died,* the performance of miracles by men in the church ceased forever.

2. *Paul tells us in Eph.* 4:8-13 *how long these gifts were to continue*: "till we all attain unto the unity of the faith, and of the knowledge of the Son of God, unto a full-grown man, unto the measure of the stature of the fulness of Christ." These gifts were to continue till the knowledge of the Son of God was completely revealed; viz., till the Scriptures were completed and confirmed. At the completion of Revelation there was no need for inspiration, nor for miracles to confirm the message.

3. *Paul*—immediately following his discussion of spiritual gifts (I Cor. 12)—*explains the expiration of such gifts*: " . . . . whether there be prophecies, they shall be done away; whether there be tongues, they shall cease; whether there be knowledge, it shall be done away. For we know in part, and we prophesy in part; but when that which is perfect is come, that which is in part shall be done away" (I Cor. 13:8-10). It is evident that these spiritual gifts were not intended for all time to come: Prophecies shall be done away; tongues shall cease; knowledge shall be done away—and there is no "maybe" about

it. When? Answer: "When that which is perfect is come" (Verse 10). They had known and prophesied God's will in part—his revelation was revealed to them a part at a time until all had been given—but when that which is perfect was come, that which was in part was done away. The perfect canon of Scriptures was completed with the book of Revelation; therefore, the miraculous gifts have ceased.

4. *The miraculous gifts of the Spirit ceased after the completion of the work for which they were given;* namely: the revelation and the confirmation of the complete will of God. To claim supernatural power today is equivalent to saying the Bible is not complete. There is no need, therefore, for the signs unless one has a new revelation to confirm. And no man has an additional revelation, for the apostles were guided into all the truth (Jno. 16:13)—not just a part of the truth—and it was completed with the book of Revelation. No man can add to it without being under the curse of damnation: "I testify unto every man that heareth the words of the prophecy of this book, If any man shall add unto them, God shall add unto him the plagues which are written in this book." There are no more revelations to confirm; therefore, there are no more signs for confirmation.

REASON XXIII

BECAUSE OF ITS SCRIPTURAL TEACHING AND OBSERVANCE OF THE LORD'S SUPPER

I. A MEMORIAL

THE church of Christ observes the Lord's supper as a sweet and simple memorial. It is a sacred and holy event in memory of Christ. Paul declares, "For I received of the Lord that which also I delivered unto you, that the Lord Jesus in the night in which he was betrayed, took bread; and when he had given thanks, he brake it, and said, This is my body, which is for you: this do in remembrance of me. In like manner also the cup, after supper, saying, This cup is the new covenant in my blood: this do, as often as ye drink it, in remembrance of me" (I Cor. 11:23-25). "In remembrance of me" is mentioned twice in this passage and once in Lk. 22:19-23. It is in memory of Christ, not only in memory of his death, but his birth, life and teaching as well, that we eat the bread and drink the cup.

We look at a flower from mother's grave in memory of man's truest earthly friend; we look at a faded picture of father in remembrance of him who guided us through tender years; we look at a lock of baby's golden hair in memory of her who was with us such a short time; we go to Washington's monument and stand with heads uncovered in memory of the father of our country; also, we gather around the Lord's table and take the Lord's supper in memory of Him who said, "This do in remembrance of me."

Hallowed flowers kept within the lids of the Bible disintegrate into fragments and powder with time; once cherished pictures are transformed by the years into unrecognizable scraps of paper; marble monuments are first effaced and finally leveled by time; but the Lord's supper is one memorial that is not disintegrated, transformed or effaced by time. Neither the grinding of the elements nor the wearing of time can keep this monument from standing in memory of Christ. Forgetting the Lord can, and this is the thing that has pulled it down in many places.

Christ commanded it to be done in memory of him. Yet many have forgotten Christ in the very thing he commanded them to do in remembrance of him. Jeremiah once said, "Can a virgin forget her ornaments, or a bride her attire? Yet my people have forgotten me days without number" (Jer. 2:32). If Jesus were speaking today, he could very easily say to the modern churches, "Can a church forget her box supper or her chili supper? Yet you have forgotten me in the Lord's supper days without number." A little investigation will establish this fact. For instance, one preacher said that in "his church" they had not observed the Lord's supper for fourteen years.

2. *It is a memorial which preaches Christ's death*: "For as often as ye eat this bread, and drink the cup, ye proclaim the Lord's death till he come" (I Cor. 11:26). Thus we see that the Lord's supper is a silent witness of the great sacrifice of all ages. Wherever it is observed, in the East, the West, the North or the South, it will present to the minds of men in a forceful way that Jesus died for them. Just as the tomb of the Unknown Soldier bears witness of the death of a soldier for his country, so the Lord's supper bears witness of the Lord's death for man. What

an effective witness   Those who fail to take the Lord's supper as God teaches, silence this witness. Such is not wise.

3. *It is a memorial which preaches the second coming of Christ*: "For as often as ye eat this bread, and drink the cup, ye proclaim the Lord's death till he come" (I Cor. 11:26). From the retrospective view, it proclaims the Lord's death. From the prospective view, it is a weekly reminder that the Lord is coming again. It points backward to his death and forward to his coming; we need the benefits derived from both that we may be ready when he comes.

4. *It is a memorial which preaches the new covenant*: "This cup is the new covenant in my blood" (I Cor. 11:25). The cup, the symbol of Christ's blood, is the sign and confirmation of a new covenant between God and man.

II. THE FREQUENCY OF OBSERVING THE LORD'S SUPPER

1. *Should there be any frequency and regularity in observing this part of the worship?* If so, who shall regulate it? The church or God? It is agreed that no man has the authority to regulate and control another's worship. This being right, the privilege, therefore, belongs to God and not man. Has God, in exercising his authority, taught one group to observe it annually, another semiannually, another quarterly, another monthly, and another weekly? Of course not. Thus it is obvious that men have stepped out of their places, usurped the authority of God, in attempting to regulate man's worship to God. In attempting to escape this conclusion men say that God has not taught us the frequency of observing the Lord's supper and that the annual, semiannual, quarterly or monthly observance is acceptable, but this lands them in another dilemma. For

if God has taught us no regular time to observe the Lord's supper, then the man who observes it only once in a lifetime has obeyed God and is just as scriptural as any one else. Hence, the Bible must have more to say about it than most people think.

2. *The Jerusalem church continued steadfastly in the observance of it*: "And they continued steadfastly in the apostles' teaching and fellowship, in the breaking of bread and the prayers" (Acts 2:42). This passage indicates a regularity and frequency and not an occasional custom. It further indicates that the frequency of its observance was so well known to Theophilus that it was useless to write him the details.

3. *The church at Troas came together on the first day of the week for the purpose of breaking bread*: "And upon the first day of the week, when we were gathered together to break bread, Paul discoursed with them, intending to depart on the morrow" (Acts 20:7). From this verse we offer the following:

(1) Their taking it on that day is an approved precedent. If it had been wrong, Paul would have condemned it.

(2) They came together on that day, the first day of the week, for the primary purpose of breaking bread. Which first day of the week? There is but one first day of the week. There has never been a week without a first day or with more than one first day.

(3) Does this mean that they took the Supper the first day of every week? It does not say "every week," but neither does it say that God commanded the Jews to keep every Sabbath. God said, "Remember the sabbath day, to keep it holy" (Ex. 20:7). They were obligated to keep the Sabbath. It came around once every week; there-

fore they were obligated to keep it every week. The early disciples met upon "the first day of the week" to break bread, and did so with apostolic approval. If we follow this approved example, how often shall we meet to break bread? Just as often as the first day of the week comes, and that is once every week.

(4) It must be admitted that the meeting together upon the first day of the week and their breaking bread, according to this verse, occurred with the same frequency. They met together upon the first day of the week, and they broke bread upon the first day of the week. Those who separate the breaking of bread upon the first day of the week from the meeting together upon the first day of the week do a thing for which they have no authority. Consistency demands that if they abandon the breaking of bread upon the first day of the week, that they also abandon the meeting together upon the first day of the week.

(5) Will those who deny that this verse teaches we should observe the Lord's supper upon the first day of every week tell us how they have learned from it that it ought to be observed annually, semiannually, quarterly or monthly?

4. *Why observe the Lord's death annually, quarterly or monthly, but observe his resurrection weekly?* All agree that the first day of the week is observed because it is the day the Lord came forth from the tomb. Now will the annual, semiannual, quarterly and monthly observers of the Lord's death—for the Lord's supper shows his death—tell us why they observe the Lord's resurrection every week but observe his death only annually, semiannually, quarterly or monthly?

5. *The church at Corinth ate the Lord's supper when*

they assembled, which was the first day of every week. To the church at Corinth, which had corrupted the Lord's supper through hunger and drunkenness, Paul said, "When therefore ye assemble yourselves together, it is not possible to eat the Lord's supper" (I Cor. 11:20). It is evident that it was their practice to attempt to eat the Lord's supper when they assembled. Now if there was any regularity about their meeting together, there was also regularity about their eating the Lord's supper. Here is the regularity about their meeting together: "Upon the first day of the week let each one of you lay by him in store, as he may prosper, that no collections be made when I come" (I Cor. 16:2). One says, "Does this mean the first day of every week?" If not, why do you pass the collection plates upon the first day of every week? If this is not your authority for it, what is? Yes, it means the first day of every week and is rendered such by Macknight. Let us see what we have: (1) It was their practice to eat the Lord's supper when they met together (I Cor. 11:20). (2) It was their practice to meet together upon the first day of every week (I Cor. 16:2). (3) Therefore, it was their practice to eat the Lord's supper upon the first day of every week.

III. WHO SHALL PARTICIPATE IN THE COMMUNION

1. *We can find out who should by finding out who did; namely*: (1) Members of the church at Jerusalem (Acts 2:42). (2) Members of the church at Troas (Acts 20:7). (3) Members of the church at Corinth (I Cor. 11:20-33).

2. *Those who are in the kingdom*: "And I appoint unto you a kingdom, even as my Father appointed unto me, that ye may eat and drink at my table in my kingdom" (Lk. 22:29,30). It is to be done in the kingdom; hence

173

only citizens of the kingdom enjoy this privilege.

3. It is the Lord's table and the Lord's supper; therefore, *only those who are the Lord's have the privilege of eating it.*

4. *However, no man or set of men has the right to judge who shall and shall not have the privilege of communion*: "But let a man prove [examine] himself, and so let him eat of the bread, and drink of the cup" (I Cor. 11:28). The self-examination taught in this verse condemns the doctrine of close communion. Each is to examine himself; not somebody else. It is an individual act of worship; it is a communion of the Christian with Christ (I Cor. 10:16); hence, it is a prerogative that belongs to Christ instead of man, because it is the Lord's table and the Lord's supper.

IV. SOME QUESTIONS

1. *Will not the frequency of communing every week destroy its solemnity?* No. There is no more foundation for this than there is to attend church only annually, semiannually, quarterly or monthly, supposing to do so oftener would destroy its solemnity and helpfulness.

2. *What is it to eat and drink unworthily* (I Cor. 11:27)? "Unworthily" is an adverb and modifies the verbs denoting the action; therefore, it has reference to the manner in which it is done, not to the worthiness of the individual. The revised version presents this thought by saying, "in an unworthy manner."

3. *What is the meaning of "the cup"* (I Cor. 11:25)? It means something they could drink, for they were told to

174

drink it; therefore, it refers to the contents and not to the container.

4. *Is the bread turned into the Lord's "actual" body; and the fruit of the vine, his "actual" blood* (I Cor. 11:25)? The Catholics think so. It is their doctrine of "consubstantiation" and "transubstantiation." They contend that the change is made today when it is "blessed" by the priest. Jesus took bread and said, "This is my body." Jesus was living in the flesh, his earthly body; so if the bread became his literal body, he had two literal bodies at the same time. Jesus also said, "This cup is the new covenant in my blood," but the cup did not become his literal blood, for such was still flowing in his veins. If it can mean nothing but the "literal" or "actual" body and blood, why insert the qualifying word "literal" or "actual"? The fact that they insert these words is proof that it could be symbolical instead of literal or actual. Why not assume that the cup is the literal new covenant? Why argue that the cup is the actual blood but not the actual new covenant? Both are in the same passage: "This cup is the new covenant." Christ also said, "I am the vine, ye are the branches" (Jno. 15:5). Why not argue that Jesus was a literal vine and the disciples were literal branches?

175

REASON XXIV

BECAUSE IT HAS SCRIPTURAL MUSIC IN THE WORSHIP

I. INTRODUCTION

A LL religious organizations are agreed that music has a place in New Testament worship, but are not agreed as to whether it should be vocal or instrumental, or vocal accompanied by instrumental; even though the New Testament, encyclopedists, historians, and commentators make plain the teaching and practice of the New Testament church.

2. The author has mentioned repeatedly that *the guiding principle in the churches of Christ* is: "Speak where the Bible speaks and be silent where the Bible is silent." A strict adherence to this basic principle is the reason for the omission of instrumental music in the worship of the churches of Christ·

II. THE MUSIC TAUGHT IN THE NEW TESTAMENT

1. *Here is the record of the music mentioned in the New Testament*: (1) "And when they had sung a hymn, they went out into the mount of Olives" (Matt. 26:30). (2) "But about midnight Paul and Silas were praying and singing hymns unto God" (Acts 16:25). (3) "Therefore will I give praise unto thee among the Gentiles, and sing unto thy name" (Rom. 15:9). (4) "I will sing with the spirit, and I will sing with the understanding also" (I Cor. 14:15). (5) "Speaking one to another in psalms and hymns and spiritual songs, singing and making melody with

your heart to the Lord" (Eph. 5:19). (6) "Let the word of Christ dwell in you richly; in all wisdom teaching and admonishing one another with psalms and hymns and spiritual songs, singing with grace in your hearts unto God" (Col. 3:16). (7) "In the midst of the congregation will I sing thy praise" (Heb. 2:12). (8) "Through him then let us offer up a sacrifice of praise to God continually, that is, the fruit of lips which make confession to his name" (Heb. 13:15). (9) "Is any among you suffering? let him pray. Is any cheerful? let him sing praise" (Jas. 5:13).

2. *Christ's leaving instrumental music out of the worship settles the matter.* The Lord's church is a New Testament institution and the New Testament tells us of the items of worship the Lord put in it. We have seen that the New Testament is silent concerning instrumental music in the worship. It is evident that those who have it in the worship do so without scriptural authority. We should not presume to add to the divine pattern.

3. *There are two kinds of commands: specific and generic.* For instance, "Make thee an ark of gopher wood" (Gen. 6:14) is a specific command. God specified the wood and that was the end of the matter relative to the kind of wood. God did not say, "Thou shalt use no other kind of wood"; but the fact that God limited the wood to gopher wood forbade the use of any other kind. Now if God had said, "Make thee an ark of wood," the use of any kind of wood would have met this generic command. Also, if the New Testament had said, "Make music," we could have complied with the requirement by making either vocal or instrumental music, or both. God, however, did not say that. He said, "sing," and that restricts the music to vocal. The specification and limitation is as clear here as it

177

was in the command to build an ark out of gopher wood. The specific command to sing should be enough for those who are willing to take God at his word and do what he says because he said it.

III. CONCLUSIONS BASED UPON MAJOR AND MINOR PREMISES

The foregoing prepares us for a further investigation of the subject. With this preparation of mind, we note the following arguments:

1. *Argument one:*

(1) Every Scripture is given that the man of God may be furnished unto every good work (II Tim. 3:16,17).

(2) No Scripture authorizes instrumental music in the worship today (cannot be found).

(3) Therefore, instrumental music in the worship today is not a good work.

2. *Argument two:*

(1) It is a violation of the Lord's will to go beyond the things which are written (I Cor. 4:6).

(2) Musical instruments in New Testament worship have not been written (cannot be found).

(3) Therefore, those who use musical instruments in the worship today violate the Lord's will.

3. *Argument three:*

(1) "So belief cometh of hearing, and hearing by the word of Christ" (Rom. 10:17).

(2) The word of Christ does not give us musical instruments in the worship (cannot be found).

(3) Therefore, instrumental music in the worship is not an act of faith.

178

4. *Argument four*:

(1) God has given us all that pertains to life and godliness (II Pet. 1:3).

(2) What God has given does not mention instrumental music in New Testament worship (cannot be found).

(3) Therefore, instrumental music in the worship today does not pertain unto life and godliness.

IV. "PSALLO"

1. Some have asked, *"Does not the Greek verb 'psallo' include playing?"* Some rest their claim upon it, but a little reasoning will cause them to give up this argument. If the original word from which we get the term "sing" implies and includes the playing of a mechanical instrument, then we cannot obey God's command to sing unless each of us in the assembly plays a musical instrument. Now who is willing to say that the playing of a mechanical instrument is included in the Greek word "psallo"? Yes, who will say that every person who attempts to worship God without playing an instrument is in rebellion to God's command?

2. *A definition of psallo.* In M. C. Kurfee's book, *Instrumental Music in the Worship,* copyrighted by the McQuiddy Printing Co., Nashville, Tennessee, p. 16, there is a summary of the definitions of the word "psallo" as given in seventeen Greek-English Lexicons, as follows:

"(1) To pluck the hair. (2) To twang the bowstring. (3) To twitch a carpenter's line. (4) To touch the chords of a musical instrument, that is, to make instrumental music. (5) To touch the chords of the human heart, that is, to sing, to celebrate with human praise."

Inasmuch as the Greek word "psallo" has carried five

different meanings at different times, what shall we say is the meaning in New Testament usage? It is clear that the meaning is "to sing," because the melody was made with the human heart: "Singing and making melody with your heart to the Lord" (Eph. 5:19). Thus the New Testament meaning is not to pluck the hair; twang the bowstring; twitch the carpenter's line; touch the chords of a musical instrument; but is to touch the chords of the human heart, for that is the instrument with which the melody is to be made.

V. DECLARATIONS OF RELIGIOUS LEADERS

Various religious leaders have written and spoken with great unanimity of thought on the music question. We now introduce some:

1. *John Calvin*, outstanding as one of the founders of the Presbyterian Church: "Musical instruments in celebrating the praises of God would be no more suitable than the burning of incense, the lighting up of lamps, the restoration of the other shadows of the law. The Papists, therefore, have foolishly borrowed this, as well as many other things, from the Jews."—*John Calvin's Commentary*, Thirty-third Psalm.

2. *Adam Clarke*, the greatest commentator of all time among the Methodists: "Music as a science, I esteem and admire: but instruments of music in the house of God I abominate and abhor. This is the abuse of music; and here I register my protest against all such corruptions in the worship of the Author of Christianity."—*Clarke's Commentary*, Vol. IV., p. 686.

3. *John Wesley*, the reputed founder of the Methodist Church, is quoted by Adam Clarke to have said: "I have no objection to instruments of music, in our chapels, pro-

vided they are neither heard nor seen."—*Clarke's Commentary*, Vol. IV., p. 686.

4. *Martin Luther*, a distinguished reformer, "called the organ an ensign of Baal"—*McClintock & Strong's Encyclopedia*, Music, Vol. VI., p. 762.

5. *John Knox*, Scottish reformer, "called the organ a 'kist' (chest) of whistles."—*McClintock & Strong's Encyclopedia*, Music, Vol. VI., p· 762.

6. *Charles H. Spurgeon*, recognized as the greatest Baptist preacher that ever lived, preached for twenty years to thousands of people weekly in the Metropolitan Baptist Tabernacle, London, England, did not have musical instruments in the worship.—M. C. Kurfees, *Instrumental Music in the Worship*, p. 196.

7. *Conybeare and Howson*, famous scholars of the Church of England, in commentary on Eph. 5:19, say, "Make melody with the music of your hearts, to the Lord . . . . . let your songs be, not the drinking songs of heathen feasts, but psalms and hymns; and their accompaniment, not the music of the lyre, but the melody of the heart."— *Life and Epistles of St. Paul*, Vol. II, p. 408.

The above religious leaders, not one of whom was a member of the church of Christ, have been quoted not for the purpose of proving instrumental music in the worship wrong—the fact that Christ left it out proves that—but to show that they have been rejected by many religious leaders of the world. If no one taught instrumental music in the worship is wrong, it would not change the New Testament teaching; but it is evident that others have occupied the same position and that we do not stand here alone by any means. Historians, encyclopedists and religious leaders are agreed that the music characteristic of the New Testament is the music characteristic of the churches of Christ.

VI. EFFORTS TO JUSTIFY INSTRUMENTAL MUSIC IN THE WORSHIP

Notwithstanding the scripturalness of vocal music in the worship, objections are offered to it and efforts are made to justify instrumental music. Some of these endeavors shall be briefly considered:

1. *Some attempt to justify instrumental music in New Testament worship by saying that it had a part in Old Testament worship.* But if that authorizes the playing of musical instruments in the worship, it will also authorize the offering of animal sacrifices and the burning of incense in the worship. If men bring instrumental music into the worship today on the ground that it is mentioned in the Old Testament, consistency demands that they bring animal sacrifices and the burning of incense also. If a man leaves the offering of animal sacrifices and the burning of incense out of the worship today on the ground that Jesus did not include them in the New Testament, he must also leave out the playing of instruments for the same reason. (That we today are living under the New Testament rule rather than the Old Testament authority, see Chapter X.)

2. *It is also said that it is right to have instrumental music in the worship because harps are mentioned in heaven.* Introducing into the worship of the church here on earth the things that are mentioned in heaven lead men into greater difficulties than they ever suspected. For instance, a verse which mentions harps also mentions "golden bowls full of incense" (Rev. 5:8). Is it right to have incense in the worship just because it is mentioned as being in heaven? No! But there is as much authority for the

incense in the worship as there is for the harp or any other musical instrument. If this incense spoken of in heaven is either literal or symbolic, it will certainly meet with my approval. And the harps that are in that celestial city, whether literal or figurative, will please me. And if God had put either the harp or the incense, or both, in the church, there would have been no objection on my part, but he has put neither in his church.

3. *Another class claims no authority for instrumental music in the worship, but insists that it is an expedient, a* thing indifferent, something that we may or may not have. If it is a matter of indifference with them, why do they not leave it out of the worship when others conscientiously object? Why insist on an expediency to the division of religious folk? Those who are indifferent to this matter are not indifferent because of a thing expedient, but are indifferent toward it as a result of their indifference to the principle of strictly holding to the divine pattern, without adding to it or taking from it.

4. *It is claimed that the use of instruments is justified because they aid the singing.* As to whether or not the instrument aids the singing depends upon the purpose for which we sing. If we make music for the purpose of entertaining the audience, putting on a show, appealing to those who have no desire to worship in spirit and truth, then the instrument perhaps will be an aid. This, however, is not the purpose of our singing. One purpose is to teach and admonish one another (Col. 3:16). Will the playing of the instrument help us to teach and admonish? No! It often drowns out the words and keeps us from being taught and admonished. Hence, it interferes

with one of the purposes for which we sing, rather than aids it.

5. *An attempt to justify instrumental music is made by saying that we occasionally use the tuning fork.* This argument is so weak that it is surely an admission that the exponent is hard pressed for proof, because musical instruments and tuning forks are not one and the same; and even if they were, it would not prove that they are acceptable to God just because we use the tuning fork. The following quotation is helpful: "Whatever is essential to doing a command is involved in the command; pitching the tune is involved in the command to sing . . . . . when a tuning fork is used to pitch the tune, nothing is done in singing that is not done without it . . . . . But when a musical instrument is used with the singing, something is done that is not done without it . . . viz., another kind of music is made simultaneously with that made by the human voice. It is praising God with two kinds of music where God himself has chosen and appointed only one kind."—Quotation from "Walking by Faith" in M. C. Kurfee's Tract, *Review of John B. Cowden's Tract on Instrumental Music in the Church*, p. 28.

6. *Occasionally we hear, "You have instrumental music at home.* If you can have it at home, you can have it in the worship." Oh, no. We have many things at home we do not have in the worship. We scrub pots and pans at home, but we do not when we assemble to worship. We eat fried chicken and gravy at home, but we only eat the bread and drink the fruit of the vine at the Lord's table. The Lord commanded the bread and the fruit of the vine, and that excludes our taking any other food at the Lord's supper; even so, the Lord has commanded us to sing, make vocal music, and that excludes any other music.

7. *It has been said, "The Bible does not say not to have it."* Does that prove that it is acceptable to God? If so, it proves that the burning of incense is acceptable; for no man can read, "Thou shalt not burn incense in the worship." It would also prove steak and hot biscuits acceptable at the Lord's supper; because no man can find the command, "Thou shalt not eat steak and hot biscuits at the Lord's supper." Such a misleading principle in religion is based upon the idea of being guided by what the Bible does not say instead of what it does say. To please God, we must be guided by what he has said, because he has warned against going beyond the things which are written (I Cor. 4:6). May we heed the warning.

REASON XXV

BECAUSE SALVATION IS IN CHRIST'S CHURCH

I. INTRODUCTION

MOST *denominational preachers say* that man does not have to be a member of the church to be saved. If they mean denominations, the institutions of which they are members, they are right. If they mean the church purchased by the blood, they are wrong.

2. *If a man can be saved out of a denomination* as well as in it, why be in it? Why preach and work to get others to be members of it, if there is no salvation in it? Such labors would not be for the purpose of saving the lost, but rather for the purpose of making proselytes to a human creed and the building up of a man-made religious fraternity in which there is no salvation.

3. *Any church which is not essential to man's salvation is not Christ's church,* because membership in his church is indispensable to salvation. This is the twenty-fifth reason that is submitted to you for being a member of the church of Christ.

II. MEMBERSHIP IN CHRIST'S CHURCH ESSENTIAL TO SALVATION

1. Salvation is in the church, because *it is the blood-purchased institution* : ". . . . . the church of the Lord which he purchased with his own blood" (Acts 20:28). Paul said to the members of the church at Corinth, "Ye are not your own; for ye were bought with a price" (I Cor.

6:19,20). That price was the blood of Christ. Let us note some deductions: (1) Church members were blood-bought; therefore, non-members were not blood bought. Who will say man can be saved apart from the blood? (2) The church is the only thing bought with the blood (Acts 20:28); therefore, those not in the church have not been blood-bought. (3) The church was purchased with the blood of Christ (Acts 20:28); therefore, if the church is a non-essential institution, God gave the blood of Christ to no avail. Every person who says that man can be saved out of the church brings an indictment against God. It is equivalent to charging God with being an unmerciful fiend who used the blood of His Son to purchase a worthless and unessential institution. We dare not in word or deed bring that charge against "the Father of mercies and God of all comfort"!

2. Salvation is in the church, for *Paul promised that Christ would save the church*: "For the husband is the head of the wife, as Christ also is the head of the church, being himself the saviour of the body" (Eph. 5:23). The body is the church (Col. 1:18). Hence, Christ is the saviour of the body or the church. This being true, what about the non-members? They are living in the world without promise or hope.

3. Salvation is in the church, because *it is there that man is reconciled unto God*: "And might reconcile them both in one body unto God through the cross, having slain the enmity thereby" (Eph. 2:16). Paul identifies the body as the church (Col. 1:18). Note the premises and conclusion: (1) It is admitted that man must be reconciled to God to be saved. (2) Reconciliation unto God is in the body or

church (Eph. 2:16; Col. 1:18). (3) Therefore, man must be in the church to be saved.

4. Salvation is in the church, because *that is the group that Christ will present unto himself*: "That he might present the church to himself a glorious church, not having spot or wrinkle or any such thing; but that it should be holy and without blemish" (Eph. 5:27). Christ is going to present the church to himself. If we are members of the church, all is well. If not, then how can we expect to be presented to Christ? Our only answer is an echo and a silence.

5. Man cannot be saved out of the church, because *God adds all the saved to it*: "And the Lord added to them day by day those that were saved" (Acts 2:47). In the King James Version we find this wording: "And the Lord added to the church, daily, such as should be saved." On that occasion three thousand were added to the church. In their lost condition they were not members, but in their saved condition they were members. Thus we see that to be saved was to be added to the church. They could not become saved without becoming members of the church. This makes it clear that the requirements of salvation and the requirements of church membership are the same. This means that all the lost are non-members, and all the saved are members. Hence, salvation is in the church, because it consists of all the saved. What about infants and mentally deficient persons? Are they in the church? No. They are safe, not saved, because they have never been lost.

6. *If one has to be a child in the family of God* to be saved, he has to be a member of God's church to be saved. This is true because Paul declares that God's family or house is God's church. "But if I tarry long, that thou

mayest know how men ought to behave themselves in the house of God, which is the church of the living God, the pillar and ground of the truth" (I Tim. 3:15). The house of God is the church of God, and the house is the family. We read of the conversion of the jailor and his house (Acts 16:29-34), but it was his family instead of his residence that was converted. We also read that Cornelius "feared God with all his house" (Acts 10:2), but it was his family instead of his dwelling that feared God. The house of God, family of God, is the church of God. If one is in the family of God, he is in the church of God. If he is not in the church of God, then he is not in the family. If he is not in the family of God, then he is not a child of God, because God does not have children out of his family. Preachers who teach that a man can be a child of God and not be a member of God's church or family are teaching that God has children out of his family and is guilty of spiritual adultery. This reproaches the name of God!

7. Jesus, the Shepherd of the sheep, taught that *man must enter the fold to be saved*: "I am the door; by me if any man enter in, he shall be saved . . . . " (Jno. 10:9). (1) Salvation is within the fold (Jno. 10:9). (2) The fold is the church (Acts 20:28). (3) Therefore, salvation is within the church.

8. Man cannot be saved out of the church, because *he cannot be saved without being a branch in the vine.* Jesus, in speaking to his disciples, said, "I am the vine, ye are the branches" (Jno. 15:5). Christ and his disciples constitute one glorious plant. Men cannot be saved apart from this plant, for Jesus said in the fifth verse, " . . . apart from me ye can do nothing."

189

9. It is impossible to be saved out of the church, because *it is impossible to be saved without being justified*:
" .... and whom he called, them he also justified ..... "
(Rom. 8:30). " .... ye were called in one body · .... "
(Col. 3:15), and the body is the church (Col. 1:18). Notice:
(1) The called are the justified. (2) The called are in the
body, the church. (3) Therefore, the justified are in the
church. This makes it plain that if man is not in the
church, he has not been justified.

10. It is impossible to be saved out of the church,
because *it is impossible to be saved without being delivered
out of the power of darkness*: "Who delivered us out of
the power of darkness, and translated us into the kingdom
of the Son of his love" (Col. 1:13). Those in the kingdom
—and the kingdom is the church (Matt. 16:18,19)—have
been delivered out of the power of darkness. Hence, those
not in the kingdom have not been delivered out of the
power of darkness. Persons out of the kingdom or
church are in need of having their eyes opened "that they
may turn from darkness to light and from the power of
Satan unto God, that they may receive remission of sins
and an inheritance among them that are sanctified by faith
in me" (Acts 26:18).

11. *Let us look at the tabernacle as a type.* There were
the holy place and the most holy place. Types can be carried too far, but it seems that the Scriptures warrant our
saying that the holy place was a type of the chrrch and
the most holy place was a type of heaven (Heb. 8, 9, 10).
The point is this: They had to go through the holy place
to get into the most holy place. Therefore, the Bible
teaches in type that man must go through the church to get
into heaven.

III. IS THE CHURCH AN UNKNOWABLE INSTITUTION

Some say, "Yes, you have to be in the Lord's church to be saved, but it is an invisible, mystical something that no human knows anything about."

This is not true: (1) It is so recognizable that three thousand were known to have been added to it on the day of Pentecost (Acts 2:41,47). They were not added until they were baptized (Acts 2:41). Therefore, God will not add unbaptized persons to it today, because he is not a respecter of persons (Acts 10:34). (2) It is so visible that a great persecution arose against it "in Jerusalem; and they were all scattered abroad" (Acts 8:1). (3) The church is so knowable in any community that we find in the New Testament several letters addressed to it in various communities: Corinth, Galatia, Thessalonica, etc.

IV. MORALITY

It is contended by some that persons with good morals, respectable citizens with clean lives, can go to heaven regardless of their relationship to Christianity.

We briefly note that if this were true:

1. Man could have been saved without Christ's coming into the world, but he came to save (Jno. 3:17).

2. One could be saved apart from Christ's stripes, but we are healed by his stripes (I Pet. 2:24).

3. A person could have been saved without the death of Christ, but he died for our sins (I Cor. 15:3).

4. Man could have been justified without the resurrection of Christ, but he was raised for our justification (Rom. 4:25).

5. We could be redeemed apart from the blood, but we have our redemption through his blood (Eph. 1:7).

6. Men could please God without faith, but without faith it is impossible to please God (Heb. 11:6).

7. One could be saved without repenting, but those who repent not shall perish (Lk. 13:3).

8. Man could deny Christ and be saved, but those who deny Christ shall be denied before the Father (Matt. 10:33).

9. A person could be saved without being baptized, but baptism saves (I Pet. 3:20,21).

10. Men could be saved without being born again, but men must be born again to see the kingdom of God (Jno. 3:5).

11. We could be saved without obeying the gospel, but Christ will render vengeance to them that obey not the gospel (II Thess. 1:8).

12. Man could be saved without being converted, but he must be converted to enter into the kingdom of heaven (Matt. 18:3).

13. We could be saved ignorant of the truth, but we must know the truth to become free (Jno. 8:32).

14. We could be saved without loving the truth, but those who love not the truth will perish (II Thess. 2:10).

15. Man could be saved apart from Christ, but apart from Christ he can do nothing (Jno. 15:5).

16. One could be saved apart from Christ's name, but there is salvation in no other name (Acts 4:12).

17. A person could be saved out of the body, but Christ is the Saviour of the body (Eph. 5:23).

18. Cornelius would have been already saved, but he was not saved until he obeyed (Acts 11:14).